THE
ALTERNATIVE
BOOK OF
RECORDS

MIKE
BARWELL

THE ALTERNATIVE BOOK OF RECORDS

W.H. ALLEN · LONDON

1984

Printed and bound in Great Britain by
Anchor Brendon Ltd, Tiptree, Essex
for the Publishers W.H. Allen & Co PLC,
44 Hill Street, London W1X 8LB

ISBN 0 491 03472 5

CONTENTS

FOREWORD

I first met Mike Barwell early in 1982 when he was partially responsible for the world's most optimistic take-over bid for a League soccer club. Mike's consortium was trying to ensure that Hull City would be rescued from the hands of a receiver, but I am convinced that the politics of the situation dictated that their gallant attempt was always to be doomed through no fault of their own. I was mirroring the developments for the *Yorkshire Post* and I gathered afterwards that the consortium had nicknamed me Claw – which is the world's most polite term possible for anyone involved in anything remotely approaching investigative journalism.

For no apparent reason whatsoever Mike and I kept in touch – normally at half-time under the main stand at Hull City's ground, which is the world's most unlikely place to hold a series of conversations about nothing in particular. The outcome of our discussions was that we inadvertently discovered that we had two other common interests – a healthy regard for the world's greatest eccentrics and deep-lying ambitions to join the company of the world's greatest authors.

Mike also told me how he was going to combine the two subjects – by producing a book on strange and silly world records. It seemed a perfectly sensible idea, so I was able to help him a little with some publicity to divert all kinds of odd claimants in his direction.

I also mentioned that I, too, had come up with a rather outrageous idea for a light-hearted book, but Mike was well ahead of me because he announced during one chat that he had gained the interest of a publisher. He also appeared to take a great delight in keeping me up-to-date with the latest records that he had unearthed – a large proportion of which always seemed to concern folk who did obscure things with their noses that many people would have considered as anti-social and many others as physically impossible. There were, of course, plenty of other applicants with equally vivid claims to alternative world records.

Those whose assertions could be verified are faithfully recorded in this book – and I hope all its readers will be as entertained as I have been by its contents and relieved to find out that not everyone in the world is dull, ordinary, boring and unimaginative.

By the way, as far as my own book is concerned, I think I must be on the verge of the world record for trying unsuccessfully to get a work published. It was, therefore, with much humility that I accepted Mike's offer to provide him with the world's worst-ever foreword to a book – and thank him at the same time for all the fun and laughs.

DAVID BOND

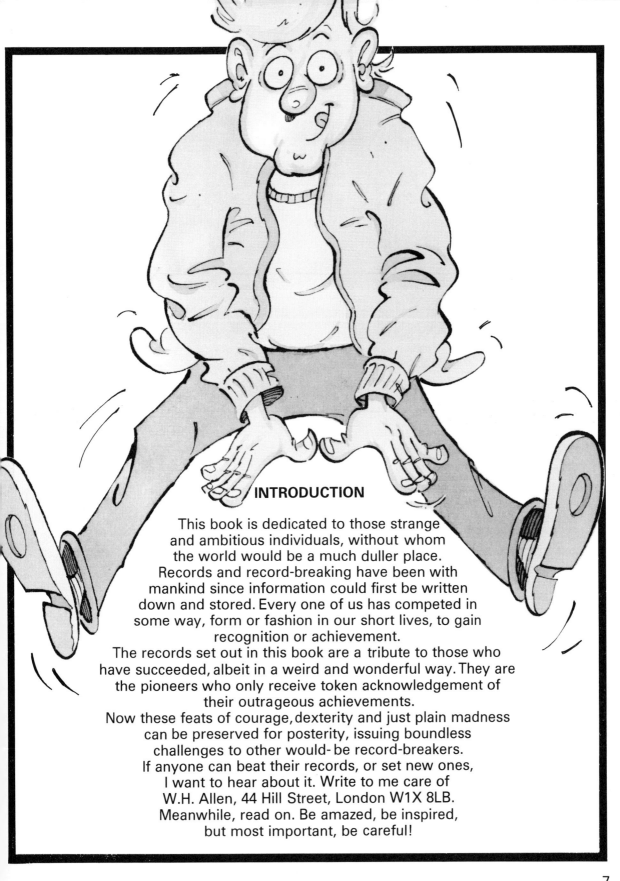

INTRODUCTION

This book is dedicated to those strange
and ambitious individuals, without whom
the world would be a much duller place.
Records and record-breaking have been with
mankind since information could first be written
down and stored. Every one of us has competed in
some way, form or fashion in our short lives, to gain
recognition or achievement.
The records set out in this book are a tribute to those who
have succeeded, albeit in a weird and wonderful way. They are
the pioneers who only receive token acknowledgement of
their outrageous achievements.
Now these feats of courage, dexterity and just plain madness
can be preserved for posterity, issuing boundless
challenges to other would- be record-breakers.
If anyone can beat their records, or set new ones,
I want to hear about it. Write to me care of
W.H. Allen, 44 Hill Street, London W1X 8LB.
Meanwhile, read on. Be amazed, be inspired,
but most important, be careful!

SPORTING RECORDS

Apple Throwing

The largest recorded distance for throwing an apple is 241 ft 6 ins achieved by Peter Stockwell of Exeter, Devon, on 29th March, 1979. The apple, a Bramley, weighed in at just under eight ounces.

Ball Kicking (Football)

On 17th February 1974 Robert Smith, aged twenty-three, of South Cave, East Yorkshire, kicked a standard, leather match-play football 212 ft from a spot kick to first bounce.

Ball Kicking (Rugby)

Roger DeVilliers, aged nineteen, kicked a standard, leather, match-play rugby football 220 ft from a place kick to first bounce on 18th February 1967 at King Edward VII playing fields, London.

Baseball

The greatest number of home runs hit in a maximum one hour period is 125. The man responsible was the irrepressible 'Babe' Ruth.

As a pre-match warm up at Wrigley Field in Los Angeles, U.S.A. in 1927, he was served by six different pitchers, hitting home runs at the rate of approximately one every 30 seconds.

Fishing – Unusual Hauls

On 21st November 1982, angler Martin Geraghty, aged twenty-nine, landed a sack full of cheques whilst fishing near his home at Wisbech, Cambs. The haul was believed to have been part of the proceeds of a robbery.

The record for the largest catch ever netted must surely go to trawler skipper, Wally Turrell, whose small fishing boat *Algerie* landed a 3,500 ton nuclear submarine off Lands End, Cornwall, in November 1982.

596

Leap-frogging

On 19th July 1974, Mike Barwell and Wally Adams, both from East Yorkshire, leap-frogged a distance of 17 miles 342 yards, at an average of one leap every five yards, along the disused railway line between Sutton and Hornsea. This sport is now banned from all respectable nudist camps.

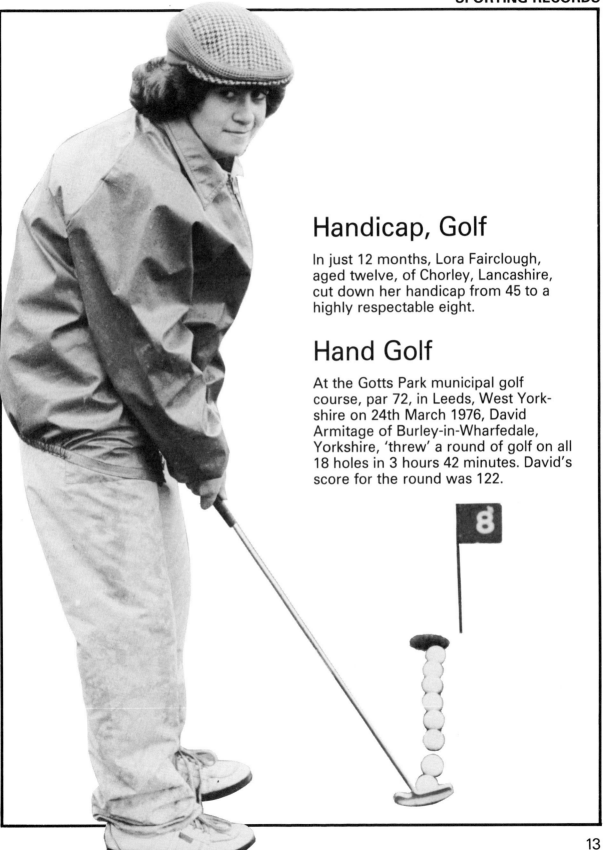

Handicap, Golf

In just 12 months, Lora Fairclough, aged twelve, of Chorley, Lancashire, cut down her handicap from 45 to a highly respectable eight.

Hand Golf

At the Gotts Park municipal golf course, par 72, in Leeds, West Yorkshire on 24th March 1976, David Armitage of Burley-in-Wharfedale, Yorkshire, 'threw' a round of golf on all 18 holes in 3 hours 42 minutes. David's score for the round was 122.

Prize Money – Boxing

The most prize money ever paid to a British boxer was £323,000 to Tony Sibsen, twenty-six, when he fought reigning World Middleweight Champion 'Marvelous' Marvin Hagler in October 1983.

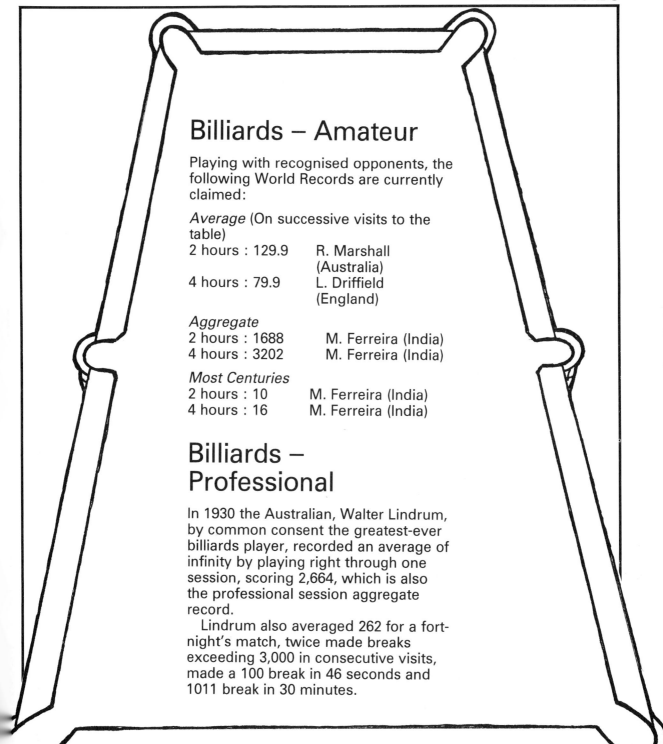

Billiards – Amateur

Playing with recognised opponents, the following World Records are currently claimed:

Average (On successive visits to the table)

2 hours : 129.9   R. Marshall (Australia)

4 hours : 79.9   L. Driffield (England)

Aggregate

2 hours : 1688   M. Ferreira (India)

4 hours : 3202   M. Ferreira (India)

Most Centuries

2 hours : 10   M. Ferreira (India)

4 hours : 16   M. Ferreira (India)

Billiards – Professional

In 1930 the Australian, Walter Lindrum, by common consent the greatest-ever billiards player, recorded an average of infinity by playing right through one session, scoring 2,664, which is also the professional session aggregate record.

Lindrum also averaged 262 for a fortnight's match, twice made breaks exceeding 3,000 in consecutive visits, made a 100 break in 46 seconds and 1011 break in 30 minutes.

Spitting

The following records were all set by Wally Adams at Thorngumbald, North Humberside, on 29th September, 1981:

1. Melon Seed   46 ft $8\frac{1}{2}$ ins
                              British record
2. Cherry Stone   48 ft $4\frac{1}{2}$ ins
                              British record
3. Grape Seed   19 ft 10 ins
                              World record
4. Peach Stone   13 ft $9\frac{1}{2}$ ins
                              World record

Roller Limbo

With the onset of the recent roller-skating revival, several new records are now up for grabs.

The ten-year-old American, Jennifer Teal, holds the current World Roller Limbo record after going clear at $6\frac{3}{4}$ inches on 1st December, 1983.

ALTERNATIVE FACT

Among the Masai tribesmen of East Central Africa, spitting is considered an act of respect and friendship.

A newborn Masai child is spat upon by close friends and relatives as a sign of good luck.

When two tribesmen meet or trade, they spit at each other as a greeting or as an acknowledgement that a deal has been struck.

Press Ups – Fingers

The following World Records are all held by Mick Gooch of Chatham, Kent. On Yorkshire Television's show *Just Amazing* Mick set a new world record for press ups on one finger by doing 40 in 46.75 seconds on 6th July, 1983.
In October 1981, at a Martial Arts demonstration in Bristol Mick accomplished:

10 press-ups on one thumb
33 press-ups on two thumbs

Skiing

French stuntman, René Petez, holds the world record for skiing through a tunnel of fire. At Alvar in the French Alps, in front of a crowd of 3,000 people, René took only eight seconds to complete the 80-yard downhill course.

Jogging

A world jogging record was claimed on 18th September, 1983, by Ron Grant, aged forty, when he completed 5,160 miles of his attempted run around Australia.

Bread salesman Ron, who runs up to 56 miles a day, aims for a total distance of 8,700 miles.

B.M.X. Riding/ Jumping

On 12th August, 1983, Dale Goodwin, aged fifteen, from Cleckheaton, Yorkshire jumped 3 Jaguar motor cars on his BMX bike. Dale attained a speed of 30 mph before hitting the sloping take-off ramp and soaring 18 ft 11 ins to clear the cars. Unfortunately, on landing Dale badly bit his tongue and had to be taken to hospital.

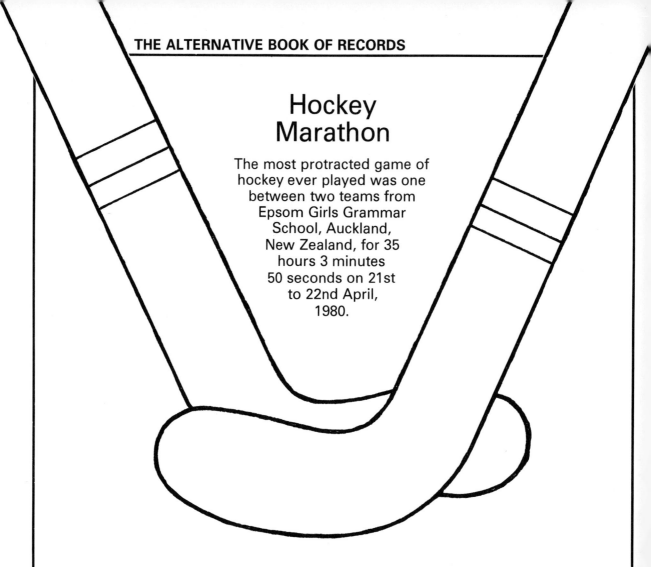

Hockey Marathon

The most protracted game of hockey ever played was one between two teams from Epsom Girls Grammar School, Auckland, New Zealand, for 35 hours 3 minutes 50 seconds on 21st to 22nd April, 1980.

Marbles

The standard size for a marble ring is 6 ft in diameter. The fastest recorded time for clearing the ring of 49 marbles is 2 minutes 57 seconds set by the 'Toucan Terribles' at Worthing, Sussex in 1971.

Walking

On 10th December, 1982, Peter Smith of Norton-on-Tees walked 138 miles non-stop in 24 hours, around the Clairville Stadium, Middlesbrough.

Worst Soccer Team

Between November 1978 and November 1982, the Second Mansfield Scouts lost all their 92 games before finally beating their 93rd opponents 4–3.

Walking on Hands (Backwards)

It was reported that on 17th February, 1975, Raymond Knopfler of Norfolk, Virginia, U.S.A. walked backwards on his hands along Main Street, a distance of 400 yards in 30 minutes exactly.

Lakes, Meres & Waters Run

Leaving Loweswater at 5 a.m. on 25th June, 1983, Joss Naylor, forty-eight, covered the 106-mile route around the Lake District in the record time of 19 hours, 14 minutes and 25 seconds. Joss dipped his hand in all 27 lakes, meres and waters and his run involved ascents totalling 18,000 ft.

Loch Ness Swim

The first swimmer to cross Loch Ness and back, non-stop, is nineteen-year-old David Morgan, from Scarborough, N. Yorkshire. David completed the 48 mile swim in 23 hours 5 minutes.

Manhattan Island Swim

On 13th July, 1983, *Oh Calcutta* actress Julie Ridge, twenty-six, became the first person to swim non-stop twice round Manhattan Island, New York, in a time of 21½ hours.

The only difficulty Julie encountered was avoiding the abundance of human effluent in the river.

Parascending

The fastest recorded time for completing a three-mile course, swooping under all 11 bridges between Lambert to Tower Bridge on the River Thames, is 26 minutes.

The record was achieved by P.C.s Gil Boyd, thirty-two, and Bob Reynolds, forty-four, in 1983.
This sponsored event raised in excess of £3,000 for the Great Ormond Street Children's Hospital.

Running – Lands End to John O'Groats

The first relay team to run the 930 miles between Lands End and John O'Groats and back again non-stop, was one comprised of ten members of the Royal Horse Artillery Regiment. The feat took a week to complete, ending on 25th August, 1983.

Sit-Ups

Chris Howson, aged twenty-seven from Darwen, Lancashire, set a new world record on 15th November, 1983, by doing 112 sit-ups in two minutes.

Shooting

In the harsh winter of 1962, on 10th January Major A.J. Coates shot and killed a record bag of 550 woodpigeon in 6 hours near Winchester, Hampshire.

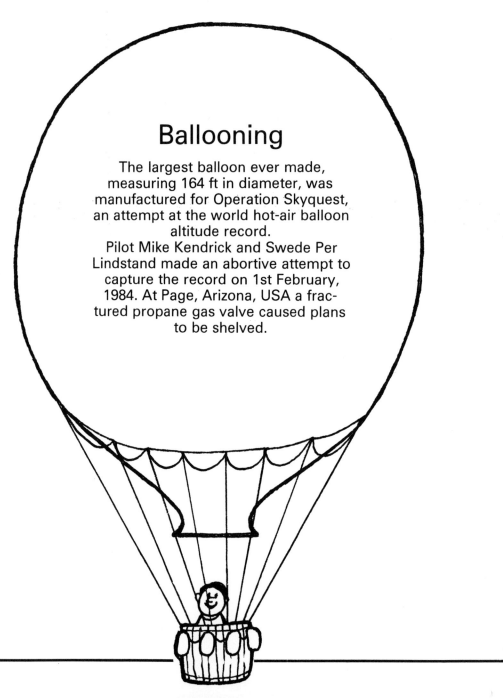

Ballooning

The largest balloon ever made, measuring 164 ft in diameter, was manufactured for Operation Skyquest, an attempt at the world hot-air balloon altitude record.
Pilot Mike Kendrick and Swede Per Lindstand made an abortive attempt to capture the record on 1st February, 1984. At Page, Arizona, USA a fractured propane gas valve caused plans to be shelved.

Bicycle Race

The most protracted non-mechanical sporting event was the 1926 Tour de France covering 3569 miles and lasting 29 days.

Sporting Record Breaker

Between 24th January, 1970 and 1st November, 1977 Russian weightlifter Vasili Alexeyev broke 80 official world records for weighlifting.

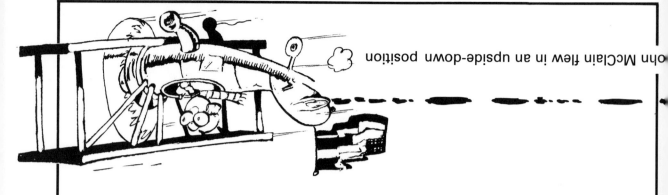

ohn McClain flew in an upside-down position

Canoeing

The fastest recorded time taken to perform 1000 'eskimo rolls' is 53 minutes 05.7 seconds, by Terry Russell at Swanley, Kent on 20th April, 1980.

Skateboard Highjump

Trevor Baxter, aged nineteen, of Burgess Hill, Sussex, holds the world high jump record of 5 ft 5.7 ins gained on 14th September, 1982, at Grenoble, France.

Skateboard Long-jump

In clearing 17 barrels, Tony Alun, aged nineteen, created a new World Skateboard longjump record of 17 ft 5 ins at the 4th U.S. Skateboard Association championships at Signal Hill on 25th September, 1977.

Basketball Marathon

At the Jordanhill College of Education, Glasgow, from 23rd to 27th March, 1981, class PE 3 played a marathon game of basketball for 90 hours 2 minutes.

Pool

According to reliable information, Michael Eufemia potted 625 consecutive balls in a ratified pool match series at Logan's Billiard Academy, Brooklyn, New York on 2nd February, 1960.

Croquet Marathon

The longest croquet match ever recorded is one of 106 hours by Craig Calvert, Andrew Cooksey, Stephen Foden and Peter Wood at Rossall School, Fleetwood, Lancashire between 1st and 5th July, 1981.

Aerobatics

On 23rd August, 1980, over Houston International Raceways, Texas USA for a total of 4 hours 9 minutes 5 seconds in a Swick Taylorcraft.

Press-ups – Flat Palms

Colin Hewick of Hull, North Humberside, holds two world press-up records:
10,029 consecutive on flat palms achieved on 18th July, 1982.
1,009 consecutive on finger tips achieved on 28th November, 1982.
Both records were set at the South Holderness Sports Centre, Preston, North Humberside.

Shortest Billiard/ Snooker Cue

The present ruling by the Billiard & Snooker Control Council is that 'a cue must be at least 3 ft in length and conform to the accepted shape & design'.

This ruling was brought about by an incident which occurred in 1938 during a professional match involving one Alec Brown. Finding the cue ball marooned in the pack of reds, he produced a tiny ebony cue, measuring $9\frac{1}{2}$ ins in length, which his father had made, with which he played his shot. His opponent protested and the resident referee, Charlie Chambers, awarded a foul which later gave rise to the aforementioned ruling.

Tandem Walkers

Denise Mitchell, aged fourteen, balanced herself atop the feet of Dave Wallbank, aged twenty-two, and together they walked tandem fashion for a distance of 4 miles between Llanwrda and Llandovery, Dyfed, Wales on 26th May, 1975.

Longest Walk

The longest walk ever undertaken by a human being was completed on 19th September, 1983 at Prudhoe Bay, Alaska USA.

Almost seven years earlier, George Meegan of Rainham, Essex, aged twenty-nine, set off from the southern-most tip of mainland South America.

Throughout his 19,021 mile trek, George occasionally met his wife, Yoshiko, at various rendezvous points. Their children were conceived on two of these occasions, and both were born before George completed his marathon.

Human Grand National

On 10th April, 1983 the headmaster of St Michael's Junior School, Kirkby, Merseyside, raised more than £6,000 for his school funds by completing the Aintree Grand National Course of 4½ miles in the record time of 40 minutes dead.

Shot Putting

Ambidextrous shot putter Allan Feuerbach holds the world record for consecutive shot puts with different hands. The total distance achieved was 121 ft 6¾ ins. The right hand put measured 70 ft 1¾ ins and the left hand put measured 51 ft 5 ins Allan performed this feat at Malmo, Sweden, on 24th August, 1974.

One-legged High Jumper

The greatest height ever cleared by a one legged high-jumper is 6 ft 8¼ ins by twenty-three-year-old Canadian, Arnie Boldt, on 3rd April, 1981 at Rome, Italy.

Underground Canoeing

On 13th January, 1983, six members of the combined Frome Canoe Club and Frome Caving Group paddled a kayak a distance of 3,000 ft through the tortuous caves and passages 400 ft under the Mendip Hills. This is the first time any journey of this nature has been undertaken.

Underwater Bike Riding

At Sheffield Swimming Baths on 20th November, 1982, a team of four 'swim-cyclers' wearing scuba gear on specially weighted bikes completed an underwater relay race (each member completing one 33-metre length) in 4 minutes 16.5 seconds.

THE WORLD OF ENTERTAINMENT

Musical Bike Riding

In the late summer of 1949, Bill Wray, aged sixteen, of Hull, East Yorkshire, rode his bicycle, 'no hands' style, a distance of three miles non-stop, whilst at the same time playing jaunty tunes on his descant recorder.

Juggling

According to reliable information, the only man in history able to juggle (as opposed to 'shower') ten balls at a time, was the Italian, Enrico Rastelli. His twenty-year career sadly ended in 1931.

Rope Tricks

The only man to demonstrate the amazing ability to spin 12 ropes simultaneously has been the American, Roy Vincent, in his career spanning from 1933 to 1953.

ALTERNATIVE FACT

The rarest trick ever performed in front of a 'Western' audience is the Indian Rope Trick.

As usually described, the rope trick is performed in India by a 'Fakir' – an Indian Holy Man.

As proof that he can perform miracles, he chants a story relating what he is doing and conjures a rope to rise from the ground which remains vertical and stiff.

He then enlists the aid of a young boy who climbs the rope and disappears from view. After a while the boy's screams are heard and then severed arms and legs fall to the ground.

The 'Fakir' gathers the limbs together and covers them with a magic cloth. When the cloth is lifted the limbs have disappeared and the boy slides back down the rope in perfect shape.

Magic or mass hypnotism? You'll never know until you've seen it.

Stand-In

The world's most unusual stand-in was found for actress Faye Dunaway – a dead pig!

To simulate the sound of a whip lashing her body, the pig was dressed in seventeenth-century attire and the subsequent tape recording dubbed over a fight scene twixt Miss Dunaway and actress Marina Sirtis during the making of the film *The Wicked Lady*.

Airlift of Bibles

In December 1982, the Bible Society despatched 100,000 Bibles, weighing a total of 69 tonnes, to Uganda.
This is the largest number of books ever to be consigned by air freight.

Television – Smallest

In November 1982 it was announced that the Japanese company Seiko had perfected a wrist watch with a one-inch square, black and white television screen and stereo radio.

Television Series

The most expensive television series ever made is the Granada Television epic *The Jewel in The Crown* at a cost of over £5,500,000.

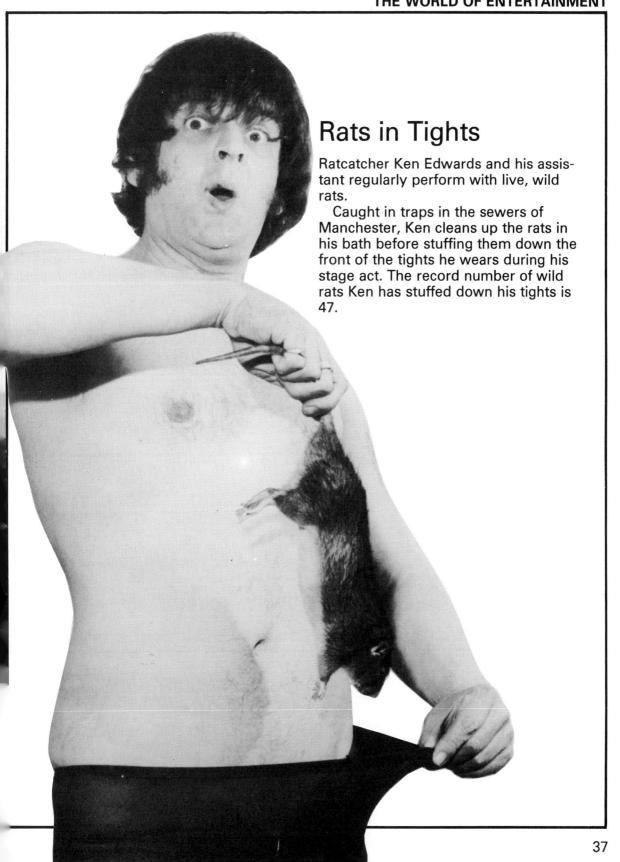

Rats in Tights

Ratcatcher Ken Edwards and his assistant regularly perform with live, wild rats.

Caught in traps in the sewers of Manchester, Ken cleans up the rats in his bath before stuffing them down the front of the tights he wears during his stage act. The record number of wild rats Ken has stuffed down his tights is 47.

Tower Fall

Stuntman and James Bond stand-in Mike Potter holds the world record for a controlled fall from a tower.

   Mike 'fell' 85 ft from a specially constructed tower onto a landing pad of foam rubber and cardboard boxes measuring 10 ft 6 ins square and 6 ft deep.

Barman – Most Unusual

In a certain Californian cocktail lounge you'll be served a wide range of aperitifs, mixers and wines by 'Jigs' the friendly chimpanzee.

   'Jigs' enjoys his work, smoking the odd cigarette and tippling red wine.

World's Worst Club Act

Unanimously voted the world's worst club entertainer at the Chalk Lane Club, Hull in 1980 was Chuffer, an impressionist.

Undefeated since then, Chuffer's favourite impressions are of farmyard machinery.

Cannon Fodder

The longest recorded time for a person to lie inside the barrel of a 16-inch-diameter cannon is 20 minutes, by Frank Pettitt, fifty-eight, of Gorton, Manchester.

Frank didn't realise he was creating this record when he unwittingly got stuck inside the barrel whilst doing maintenance checks.

Juggling Hedgehogs

Alexander Poskitt of Newtown, Powys, Wales has claimed to be the only person able to juggle four live hedgehogs with ungloved hands.

Recording Contract

The Rolling Stones hold the record for clinching the biggest recording deal in history. In August 1983 they signed with American CBS Records in a deal ensuring a £28 million pay-out to the British pop group.

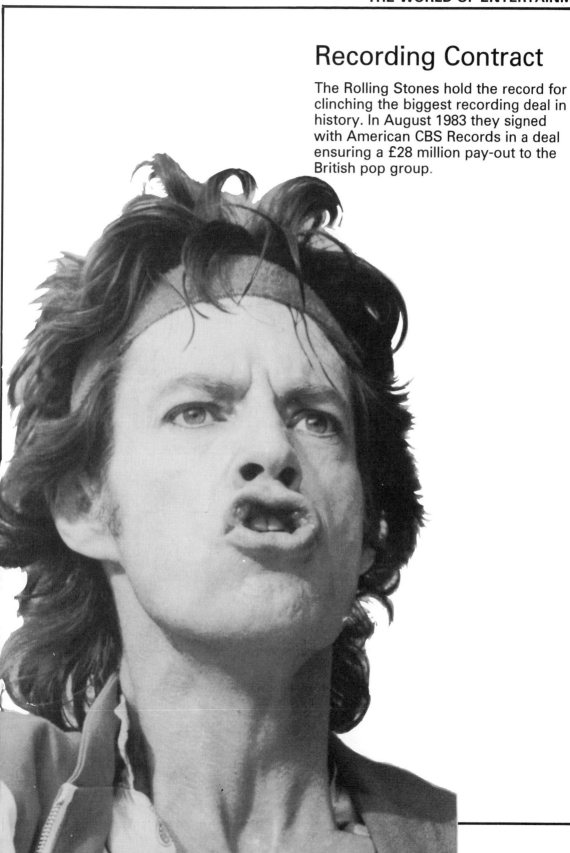

Louie Louie Louie Louie

For 63 solid hours, ending on 25th August, 1983, the radio station KFJC-FM in Berkeley, California, continually broadcast the 20-year-old rock-'n'-roll number 'Louie Louie'.

Some 800 renderings were broadcast, most of them the painful offerings of the station's listeners.

The lesser known performers included The Bowl of Slugs, The Bloodclots and Little Nymph and the Spectonettes.

One-legged Bicycle Diving

The greatest recorded height from which a one-legged (or two-legged for that matter) person has dived, remaining seated and upright on a bicycle until 'splash down' is 95 ft.

In 1902 a twenty-three-year-old American, simply called Mr Gifford, would perform this feat twice daily at the London Hippodrome diving from a platform under the roof into the flooded arena.

Stunt – Most Expensive

The most expensive stunt (in terms of the fee paid to a stunt man) was performed by Roy Allen.

Roy was paid a cool one million dollars for his stunt in the making of the film *The Curse of the Pink Panther*. For his money, Roy had to fall backwards into the sea, seated in a wheelchair, with his leg in plaster, firing a bazooka!

Shooting

Whilst touring Germany with her rodeo in the early part of this century, legendary markswoman Annie Oakley was challenged by Crown Prince William to shoot the end off a cigarette held between his lips.

   Not wanting to shoot too close to the Prince's face, Annie obliged by just shooting away the ash, leaving the cigarette still alight. She did this from a distance of 100 ft.

Comic Strip

The longest-running current comic strip still printed is the *Katzenjammer Kids*. The adventures of Hans and Fritz first appeared in the *New York Journal* on 12th December, 1897 and are still published in several American periodicals.

Stage Performance

Surely the most outrageously funny stage act ever was that performed by Joseph Pujol, 'Le Petomane'. At the famous Moulin Rouge, Paris between 1892 and 1900 he entertained millions by passing wind on a variety of musical notes and so playing tunes which included a rendering of the French national anthem.

In addition, again using only 'wind power', Pujol could blow out a candle at a distance of one foot.

At private functions, completely naked, he would plunge his bottom into a big container of water on the ground, and using his sphincter muscles he would then draw up a large quantity of water through his anus into his large intestine. Then removing himself from the container, he would bend over and expel the water with such force that he could knock over skittles at a distance of four metres.

ALTERNATIVE FACTS

The most extreme case of compulsive coin swallowing was one recorded by Sedgefield General Hospital, County Durham on 5th January, 1958.

A fifty-four-year-old man, admitted complaining of severe stomach cramps, was found to have a total of 424 coins in his stomach – 366 half-pennies, 11 pennies, 17 three-penny bits, 26 sixpences, and 4 shillings.

In addition doctors also discovered 27 pieces of wire, totalling 5 lb in weight.

Human Regurgitator

The only acknowledged human regurgitator able to 'bring back' swallowed objects on command (and in the case of multiple swallowings, in requested order) is Scotsman Stevie Starr.

Stevie practised and perfected this unusual act during his upbringing in an orphanage, when he conceived the idea that the safest place to keep his pocket money was in his stomach.

OUTRAGEOUS ACHIEVEMENTS

Bed of Glass

On 13th February, 1982, Barry Silver of Manchester, lay on a bed of broken glass cullet with a 2,100 lb weight, spread evenly over a board, on his chest.

Bed of Nails – Duration

The duration record for lying on a bed of un-blunted six-inch nails is held by Reg Morris of Walsall.
Between lst and 9th April, 1983 he lay non-stop on a bed of nails for 200 hours 5 minutes.

Bed of Nails – Greatest Weight

On BBC Television's *Late, Late Breakfast Show* on 10th December, 1983, John Kassar lay prone on a bed of unblunted six-inch nails.
A wooden board was placed on his chest and 29 girls climbed onto it. The total weight pressing down on John's body was 1 ton 12 cwt 3 stone 12 lbs (3638 lbs). Although his body was marked, the unblunted nails did not penetrate the skin.

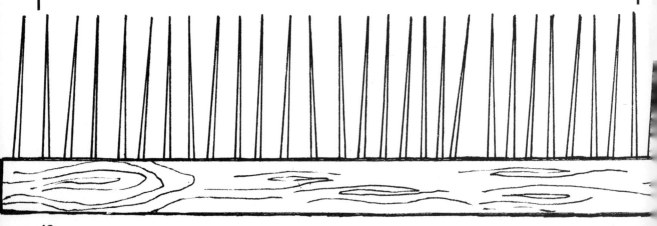

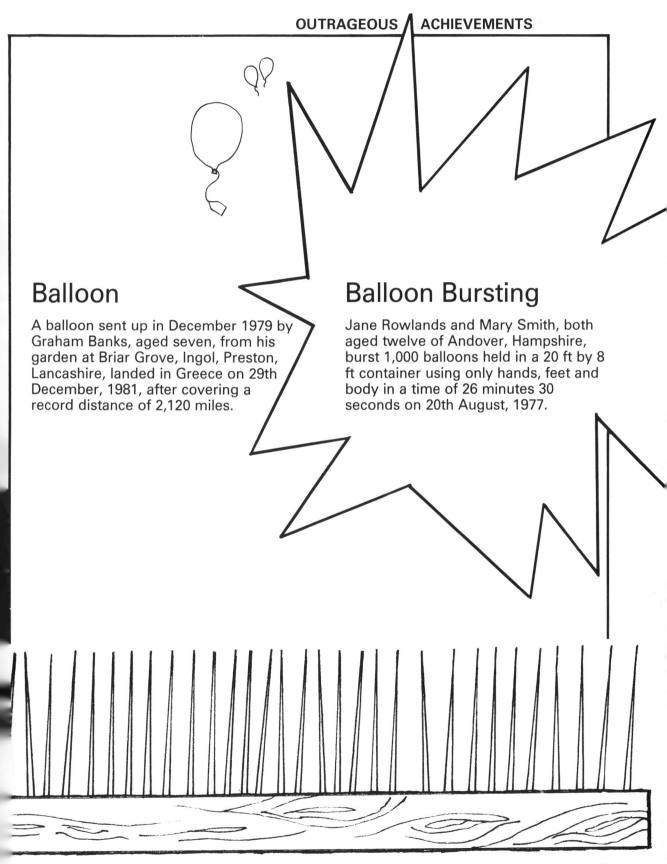

Balloon

A balloon sent up in December 1979 by Graham Banks, aged seven, from his garden at Briar Grove, Ingol, Preston, Lancashire, landed in Greece on 29th December, 1981, after covering a record distance of 2,120 miles.

Balloon Bursting

Jane Rowlands and Mary Smith, both aged twelve of Andover, Hampshire, burst 1,000 balloons held in a 20 ft by 8 ft container using only hands, feet and body in a time of 26 minutes 30 seconds on 20th August, 1977.

Balancing

Paul Harbet of Warrington is reported to have balanced, unsupported, on one leg atop a £1 stack of half-crowns (eight coins) for a period of one minute on 2nd January, 1969. Future attempts at this record will be accepted using decimal coinage.

Bond Signing

On 22nd September, 1978, Salvation Army Major George D. Thomas signed 12,551 specially prepared Charity Bonds in 16½ hours outside a supermarket in Hull, East Yorkshire.

The bonds were on sale to the general public and George raised £138.50 for his charity.

Bath of Spaghetti

As part of a money raising stunt for 'Panto' week, Liverpool University student Philip Yarrow sat in a bath full of cooked spaghetti for 100 hours 10 minutes from 14th to 18th February, 1983.

During the marathon Phil wore various funny costumes and the spaghetti had to be changed three times because it kept going rancid.

Bath of Porridge

During the winter of 1983, Michael Weston, twenty-two, of Crewe, Cheshire raised £147 for charity by sitting continuously in a bath of cold porridge for 72 hours.

Unfortunately, instead of handing over the sponsorship cash, Michael pocketed the lot and was ultimately given 90 days 'porridge' by the local magistrate.

Ball Balancing

Amateur soccer player Trevor Foster of Wath-upon-Dearne, Yorkshire, claims to have walked 200 yards in one minute whilst balancing a soccer ball in the pit of his neck on 29th April, 1980.

Bed Race

The record time for completing the annual 'Knaresborough Bed Race' is 13 minutes 28 seconds by the ICI Fibres Flying Fiasco team.

   Held annually in North Yorkshire, the bed race course crosses the river Nidd and is two miles in length.

Beer Crate Racing

Carrying a full, 12-pint crate of beer bottles, weighing 30 lbs twenty-two-year-old Lee Whiting covered a measured half mile course in four minutes 11 seconds on Ist May, 1983.

Brick Carrying

The holder of the marathon brick carrying record is Peter Dowdeswell of Earls Barton, Northants.

   For a distance of 54 miles, Peter carried a standard four pounds eight ounces house brick in the same ungloved hand in a downward position.

Bubble

The biggest bubble ever made was produced by Katherine Harting on BBC TV's *Show Me Show* on 14th September, 1983.

Using a piece of wire bent into a circular shape and a strong solution of soap suds, Katherine produced the mammoth 46.8 centimetres diameter bubble.

Bus Jumping

The greatest number of double-decker buses cleared by a motor-cyclist is 18.

This feat was achieved by twenty-five-year-old Chris Brownham at Bromley, Kent on 29th August, 1983.

Brownie

The oldest person to join the Brownies was Helen Moss of Bicester, Oxfordshire, who at the age of eighty-six was admitted to her first pack on 9th October, 1983.

Camel in a Cesspit

This innocuous record was unwittingly set by an unsuspecting creature in Ryadh, Saudi Arabia in June 1981. The cesspit had become covered over with a layer of drifting sand when the camel wandered into it.

It took six hours to pull the camel to safety at a compound cost in men and machinery of £5,000. When finally rescued, the ungrateful beast shook itself vigorously, so sharing its coating of shh, you know what, with its rescuers.

Brick Lifting

In March 1980, Fred Burton of Cheadle, Staffs laid claim to this record by lifting 24 common house bricks, each 8 ins x 4 ins x 2½ ins and weighing a total of 112½ lbs side by side in a clamp position.

Car-Cramming

Because of the vast number of makes of vehicles on the road today, it is impossible to list all the car-cramming claims. The record for a Ford Sierra stands at 27 people, achieved in October 1982 by students at the University of Nottingham.

The record for a Metro stands at 21 achieved by members of the Plymouth Young Wives association at Devonport, Devon on 30th September, 1982.

The record for a Volkswagen 1300 is 34 achieved by members of Chelsea College, Eastbourne, Sussex on 15th February, 1969.

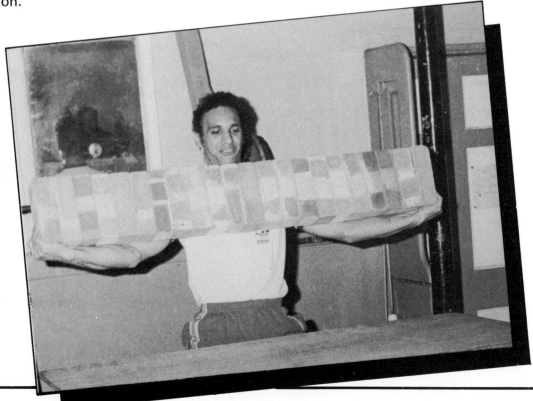

Cigars – Most in Mouth

On 16th May, 1971 at the Cock and Bell public house, Preston, East Yorkshire, landlord John Robinson crammed 25 full size Castella cigars into his mouth. All John's teeth are his own and no false ones were removed to create this record.

Card Signing

Salvation Army Major George D. Thomas signed 9,000 cards in aid of charity in a 12-hour session on 25th June, 1977 at Holywood Arches, Belfast, Northern Ireland.

Cigar

It would take about three and a half years non-stop puffing to smoke the world's largest cigar.

Manufactured from 15,903 tobacco leaves by Garcia Brothers in Las Palmas, Canary Islands, 12 ft 6 ins of pure Havana tobacco weighing more than 4 cwt, it now takes pride of place in a tobacconist's window in the Hague, Holland.

Crane Fishing

On 7th February, 1982, after exactly one hour of angling, Geoff Andrew of Edenthorpe, Yorkshire, finally got a bite. Using a 7-tonne mobile crane, Geoff landed a ten-year old Morris Marina Car.

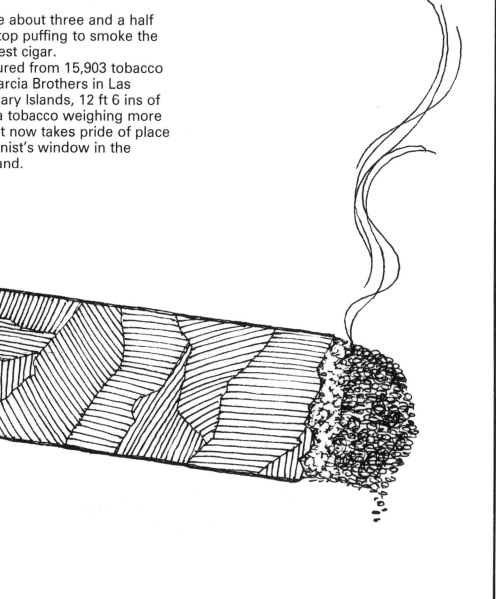

Cannibals (British)

During the fifteenth century the cannibalistic, cave-dwelling Bean family from Galloway, Scotland are reported to have murdered and eaten more than 800 victims over a 20-year period. They were finally captured and executed en masse in Edinburgh.

According to Professor Brian Simpson, a lecturer in law at Kent University, cannibalism was widespread among sailors during the last century.

It was an accepted practice, in times of extreme hunger and hardship, to draw lots to see which man would be eaten.

Professor Simpson cites one case in particular where; 'Captain Tom Gorman of Limerick who had consumed his apprentice in the approved manner in 1836, remained a respected member of the community until he retired in the early 1860's.'

Car Jump – Longest Attempted

The longest jump ever attempted in a four-wheel vehicle was by Ken Powers the U.S. stunt-driver.

In his ultra-tuned, fuel injected, 1976 Lincoln Continental, Ken attempted to jump the one mile distance from Morrisburg, Ontario, Canada across the St Lawrence River to Ogden Island, USA.

The site and specially-built take off ramp took four years to prepare, involving the movement of 110,000 cubic yards of earth. The car left the ramp at a speed of 280 mph and soared (momentarily) to a height of 305 ft before a safety parachute prematurely opened, causing the car to disintegrate and plummet into the river.

Fortunately Ken escaped injury.

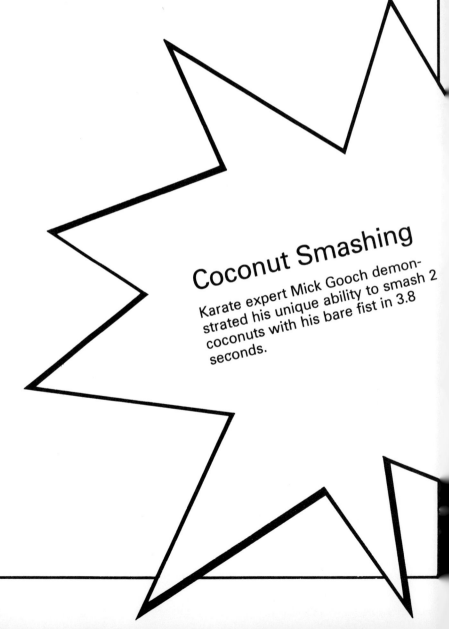

Coconut Smashing

Karate expert Mick Gooch demonstrated his unique ability to smash 2 coconuts with his bare fist in 3.8 seconds.

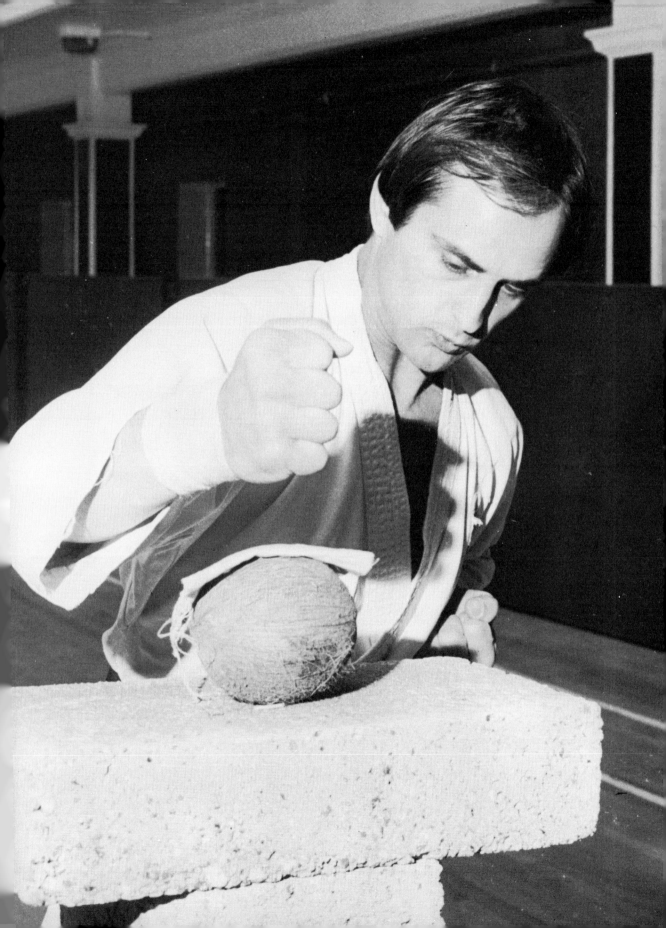

Coin Balancing

The greatest number of 12-sided, threepenny pieces balanced edge on edge is ten, claimed by Ivan P. Polumin at Godalming, Surrey on 17th September, 1961.

Car and Caravan Jump

Frenchman Gerard Stoeckli achieved a record distance of 75 ft whilst clearing 15 parked cars and towing a 14 ft caravan. The jump might have been somewhat shorter, had not the caravan landed on top of the towing car, which somersaulted in the air.

Car Jumping

American Steve Lewis regularly jumps longitudinally over approaching cars travelling at 70 mph.

Steve's attempt at jumping two cars, travelling at 100 mph was less successful. His foot hit the window-screen of the first vehicle, and was ripped off. Luckily surgeons managed to sew his foot back on again and Steve will attempt the same feat some-time during 1984.

Bottle-Opening Octopus

A friendly octopus, cared for by 17 year-old Nicholas Kruger of Port Elizabeth, South Africa has been trained to uncork bottles containing tasty crabs. The record time for opening the bottles is 14 seconds.

Concrete Block Smashing

Whilst serving a 35-year sentence in Pault Correctional Institution, Florida USA martial arts expert Willie James Washington smashed his way to a new world record. Using only his head, Willie smashed a pile of $1\frac{1}{4}$ ins thick concrete blocks. The blocks were separated by pencils $\frac{1}{4}$ in thick and the total height of the target was 18 ins.

THE ALTERNATIVE BOOK OF RECORDS

Debating

The longest record that a debate has ever been continued for is 72 hours, by two teams of students from the University of Glasgow, Scotland. It has long been forgotten exactly what they were supposed to be arguing about.

Custard-Filled Wellies

On 16th August, 1977 Stuart McIver of Hawick, Scotland ran a measured mile in the time of 6 minutes, 20.2 seconds wearing a pair of custard-filled wellies.

Custard Pie – Biggest

The biggest custard pie ever made was one measuring 36 ins in diameter weighing just short of 18 lbs by six pupils from Clayton Secondary Modern School, Oxford on 14th April, 1965.

Cue Lifting

Jim Mills lifted 24 16 oz billiard cues simultaneously, holding only the tapered tips, from the vertical to the horizontal (through 90 degrees) at Alfreton Park, Derbyshire on 13th June, 1982.

Jim went on to lift a 22 oz cue 1005 times consecutively by the same method.

Airplane Pulling

The longest recorded distance for pulling a 77-tonne Concorde airplane, using only muscle and strong ropes, is 880 yards by a team of 200 at Duxford airfield near Cambridge, England on 6th February, 1983.

Defector

On 30th August, 1983, a forty-six-year-old Chinese Air Force pilot was presented with £2½ million in gold by the Taiwan Government. His payment was for defecting from the People's Republic of China and taking his MiG 21 jet fighter plane with him.

Cue Throwing

The greatest reported distance that a 17½ oz billiard cue has been thrown, javelin fashion, is 148 ft 4 ins by Jack Bort of Newcastle, Tyne and Wear on 24th January, 1959.

Champagne Fountain

On 19th April, 1983 Carl Groves broke his own world record for stacking and filling champagne glasses. Carl and a willing assistant successfully filled 23 champagne glasses, stacked atop of each other at Richmond, Victoria, Australia.

Fistful of Money

On 27th June, 1969, Harry Bennett, seventeen, of Newport, Isle of Wight, balanced £12 worth of half crowns (96 coins) in his hand for a period of one minute.

Future attempts will be accepted using decimal coinage.

Egg Balancing – Aquatic

Aboard the motor vessel *Target Venture* at Selby, Yorkshire, Fred Daltry, a cook, successfully balanced 15 fresh hens eggs in the palm of his hand, keeping them steady for 30 seconds.

Sheep in a Snowdrift

An overweight sheep (now nicknamed Snowdrift) has survived a record 45 days trapped in a snowhole at her owner Dugald Wyper's farm at Cushnie, Aberdeenshire.

Fit, but much slimmer, Snowdrift was dug out on 8th March, 1984 after the snow had melted sufficiently (from its original depth of 10 ft) to expose her ears.

Ferret Legging

Albert Miskin, aged forty-four, from Macclesfield, Cheshire, claims to be the world champion ferret legger.

On several occasions Albert has stuffed live ferrets down his trousers, the longest durations for which are 10 minutes 30 seconds for 2 ferrets (one down each leg)and 5 minutes 10 seconds for 4 ferrets (2 down each leg)

During record attempts, no undergarments can be worn and the trouser bottoms must be firmly secured with string.

Penny Plonking

Six children from Lanark Primary School are claiming a record for throwing new pennies from a distance of 10 ft into a 2½ gallon plastic bucket. In 15 minutes they succeeded in throwing a total of 895 pennies into the bucket.

Flying Deckchair

By attaching 42 gas-filled weather balloons to a deckchair Larry Walters of Los Angeles, California soared to a height of 16,000 ft before landing again.
His controlled descent was made by bursting some of the balloons with an air pistol.

During the course of his hour long-flight, Larry was buzzed by a reconnaissance aircraft which had been alerted following a UFO report.

67

Paydeal – Longest Negotiation

Negotiations lasting 40 years came to a profitable conclusion on 19th October, 1983 for a group of 854 Aborigines, who helped to man Australia's defences during World War Two.

They claimed that they should have received the same rate of pay as white troops instead of just half the rate. In conceding that the Aborigines' claim was just, the Australian Government have agreed to pay a total of £4 million to the 854 Thursday Islanders over the next 3 years.

Bankruptcy Payout

The smallest payout ever recorded by a bankrupt was agreed by accountants appointed to sort out the business interests of William Stern, aged forty-eight, who was declared bankrupt in February, 1979 to the tune of £148 million. Creditors will get a dividend of 0.0018 on the pound, about 2,000th of a penny, with effect from 5th September, 1983.

Woggle Hopping

The art of Woggle Hopping –vaulting over pillar boxes – originated in South Yorkshire in the 1940s and is still a popular pastime to this very day. The greatest number of woggle hops achieved in one minute is 8, by Herbert Walker of Sheffield. The greatest number of woggle hops performed in one hour is 138 by David Ackroyd, aged twenty-two, of Chesterfield on 16th November, 1962.

Egg Jumping

Tony McAbe of Manchester is the only known exponent of the art of egg jumping. So nimble and light footed is Tony that he can jump on an egg and off again without breaking it.

Piano Playing Balloonist

In November 1983, John Briggs of Bingley, West Yorkshire, set a new world record for piano playing.

At a height of 4,000 ft in a Hot Air Balloon, John played merry tunes on an upright piano, thereby raising £3,500 for charity.

Tortoise – Oldest Mother

A seventy-year-old tortoise belonging to a family in Lowestoft, Suffolk, became a mother when 6 of her eggs hatched out on 10th March, 1984.

ALTERNATIVE FACTS

The world's first toothbrush was invented in 1770 by William Addis.

Addis was serving a six month prison sentence at Newgate Prison, London, for inciting a riot when he decided it was time he made a better life for himself.

In those days it was common practice to clean one's teeth with a rag or a piece of wool. Addis decided he would try to improve on this.

One evening he secreted a small-bone out of the prison mess hall and on the way back to his cell stole some stiff bristles from a sweeping broom.

All night Addis laboured, boring small holes in the bone and tying tufts of bristles in place until he had a toothbrush; not very different in style to that of today.

When Addis was released he started a manufacturing business which has now grown into a highly profitable and very rich company.

Streaker – World's First

According to reliable information (*New English Bible*, St Mark, Chapter 14, verses 51–52) the world's first streaker was 'a young man with nothing on but a linen cloth. They tried to seize him but he slipped out of the linen cloth and ran away naked'.

Teeth Cleaning Marathon

Pauline Mortimer, aged 14, set a new world teeth cleaning record on 22nd August, 1981 when she cleaned her teeth continuously for 8 hours 30 minutes.

Speeding Motorist

The first man to be prosecuted and fined for speeding was Walter Arnold, a miller of Paddock Wood, Tonbridge, Kent. On 28th January, 1896, at a time when the speed limit was 2 mph, the dashing Mr Arnold was racing along at a reckless 8 mph when he happened to pass the local constable's house. The policeman leapt on his bicycle in hot pursuit and managed to arrest the driver after a five-mile chase. The tearaway Arnold was fined one shilling.

Eiffel Tower Flyer

The first (and hopefully the last) man to try to fly from the Eiffel Tower was inventor Franz Reickatt.

Franz had invented a special loose-fitting coat with voluminous folds of cloth which he claimed would be able to support him in such a fashion that he would glide safely to the ground.

In 1912, from a platform 190 ft up the Eiffel Tower, Franz (after much hesitation) tried out his invention and plummeted to his death. After impact, his mutilated body was found to have made a 15 cm depression in the hard earth below.

Free-fall Motorcyclist

The world's first and only free-fall
motorcyclist is American stunt man
Jimmy Davis, who drove his motorbike
out of the cargo hold of a transport
plane at a height of 7,000 ft.

Rider and bike parachuted safely to
the ground, with the bike still ticking
over, landed and accelerated away as
Jimmy detached the parachute.

Flat Cap Throwing

At the annual World Champion Flat Cap Throwing contest held at the Princes Royal Hospital, Sutton, Hull, North Humberside, Territorial Army Private Kevin Anthony Cowles, achieved a distance of 79 ft 7 ins on 10th September, 1983.

Accordion Playing

Starting at twelve noon on 4th August, 1982, Tom Luxton of Oldbury Warley, West Midlands played his accordion continuously for a total of 84 hours ending at twelve midnight on Saturday 7th August, 1982. Tom's marathon was performed at the Robin Hood public house at Quarry Bank, West Midlands and raised over £3000 to buy a heart monitoring machine for Wolverhampton Hospital.

Kissing – Number of Women

As a healthy contribution to Newcastle University's Community Action Week, Jonathan Hook kissed 4106 women in 8 hours.

Mileage Record

On 1st March, 1984 it was reported that a Volkswagen car bought new in 1950 by Mr Tony Levy of Ickenham, Middlesex had clocked up a total mileage of 767,000.

Can you prove that your car has travelled further?

Mass Vasectomies

The largest number of vasectomies undertaken at the same time for a specific cause, took place on 8th February, 1983. To celebrate the 55th birthday of their monarch, King Bhumibol, 714 Thais had vasectomies.

Spokesman for the organising committee, hydroplane captain and father of 22, Mr Li Dong Seng, said 'I was inspired by the song 'I'm Vasecto-mised' which is No. 3 in our top twenty.'

Pipe Smoking

The duration record for keeping a pipe alight, using only one ounce of tobacco and one initial match, is claimed by Yrjö Pentikainen of Kuopio, Finland. Yrjö's marathon lasted 4 hours 13 minutes 28 seconds from 15th – 16th

Sneezing

The greatest number of genuine sneezes recorded in a 12-hour period is 12,000 during a sneezing bout, still continuing as at 31st January, 1984. The victim is 22 year-old Adam Cronin of London who began sneezing on 14th November, 1983 at 5 a.m.

Fortunately, Adam's sneezing ceases as darkness falls or if he sits in a dark room.

Radio Phone-Ins

Max Nottingham of Lincoln, claims to hold the world record for the most successful caller to radio phone-ins. During 1983 he successfully aired his views and chatted 264 times on 12 different stations.

House of Cards

The greatest height to which a house of cards has ever been built is 11 ft 10½ ins by Ian Nussbaum of London at a Chelsea church.

The task took Ian 14 days to complete and he used over 10,500 playing cards, all bought at his own expense.

Grape Catching (solo)

The greatest distance ever achieved for throwing and catching a grape in the mouth is 39 ft 6 ins by Camilo Antonio Mendez at Folkstone, Kent on 14th January, 1980.

Grape Catching (duo)

On 14th October, 1979, Geoff Flounders of Salford, Manchester caught a grape in his mouth thrown 187 ft by his brother, Peter.

Hot Water Bottle Bursting

The record for blowing up a hot water bottle to its maximum extendable circumference before it bursts is held by Fred Burton, of Cheadle, Staffordshire with a measurement of 8 ft exactly.

Face Slapping

The endurance record for face slapping is held by two Russians, Vasiliy Bezbordny and Gonivisch who in Kiev in 1931 slapped each other continually for 30 hours before the contest was declared a draw.

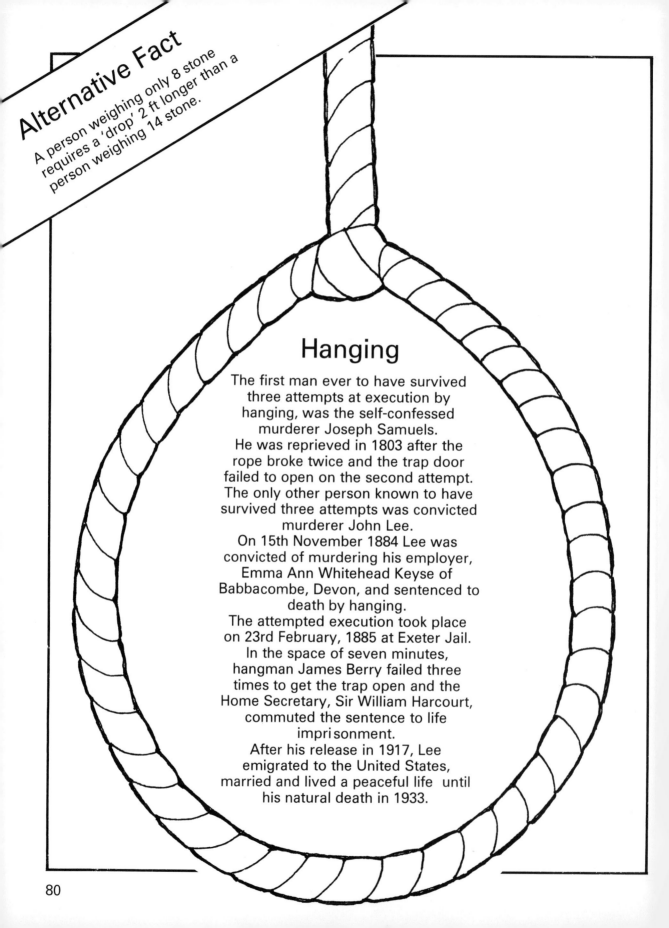

Alternative Fact

A person weighing only 8 stone requires a 'drop' 2 ft longer than a person weighing 14 stone.

Hanging

The first man ever to have survived three attempts at execution by hanging, was the self-confessed murderer Joseph Samuels.
He was reprieved in 1803 after the rope broke twice and the trap door failed to open on the second attempt.
The only other person known to have survived three attempts was convicted murderer John Lee.
On 15th November 1884 Lee was convicted of murdering his employer, Emma Ann Whitehead Keyse of Babbacombe, Devon, and sentenced to death by hanging.
The attempted execution took place on 23rd February, 1885 at Exeter Jail.
In the space of seven minutes, hangman James Berry failed three times to get the trap open and the Home Secretary, Sir William Harcourt, commuted the sentence to life imprisonment.
After his release in 1917, Lee emigrated to the United States, married and lived a peaceful life until his natural death in 1933.

Igloo Marathon

Mystic Jim Randi, forty-six, entombed himself unclad in an ice igloo, under strict medical surveillance for 43 minutes 8 seconds in Boston, Massachusets, USA, on 31st August, 1974.

Ironing

In Melbourne, Australia, on 9th March, 1973, Mrs J. Maasen, thirty-seven, completed the longest-recorded ironing marathon of 89 hours 32 minutes.

Hamburger Heaving

Using a full sized Chinese wok (a bowl-shaped frying pan) Trevor Tass, twenty-four, of San Francisco, USA is reported to have propelled a half pound, cooked hamburger 'sling shot' fashion a distance of 80 yards.

ALTERNATIVE FACT

The largest and heaviest hamburger ever made was in Australia in 1975. It measured 27 ft 6 ins in circumference and weighed 2,859 pounds.

Driving Test Passes

Triplets, Mark, Paul and Nigel Ashley, aged seventeen, of Ellerton, Sambrook, Shropshire, set a new world record between 8th and 9th June, 1983, when, in the space of 23 hours 30 minutes, they all successfully passed their driving tests at the first attempt.

High Altitude Morris Dance

Keith Naylor, twenty-five, of Laughton, Yorkshire holds the world record for morris dancing at a height of 20,000 ft. On a climbing expedition to the Himalayas Keith's feat was performed close to the summit of Mount Cholaste in June, 1983.

Hopping

Alex Smith, eighteen, of Corby, Northants, hopped on one leg a distance of one mile around Banbury High School playing fields in the record time of 29 minutes 58 seconds on 27th April, 1972.

Human Mole

In 1974, fearing further extensive questioning by police regarding a case of rape, Norman Green of Ince, Wigan, Lancashire hid himself away under the floor boards of his house.

Eight years later, in July 1982, very pale and weak, Mr Green emerged to find that the police had long since ruled him out of their enquiries.

Throughout the years Mr Green had been fed and cared for by his wife Pauline, the only person who knew of his whereabouts.

ALTERNATIVE FACT

A mole can dig tunnels underground at the same speed as it can run above ground.

Growth Rate

According to reports received from Spain on 14th February, 1983, an 18 month-old baby in Murcia has amazed doctors with his growth. Abraham Munoz, who weighed 9 lb at birth was as big as a four year old, tipping the scales at 2 stone 11$\frac{1}{2}$ lbs and was 3 ft 1 in tall.

Knitting

Bill Fairman of Peterborough set a new world record for non-stop knitting of 336 hours, finishing his marathon on 18th December, 1981.

Longest Hair

Hotel housekeeper, Dhorie Geronima, thirty-eight, from Earls Court, London, has the longest hair in Great Britain. As at 1st January 1984, her tresses measured 65¾ ins from head to ankles.

Loop the Loop

Pilot Ken Ballinger, thirty-five of Painswick , Gloucestershire claims to have looped the loop 155 times in one hour in his light aircraft.

Lorry landing

The only known exponent of the art of landing a Piper J3 Cub aircraft on the top of a moving lorry is American stunt man, Art Shorn, of California USA. Guided by fellow stunt man, Larry Hall, Art lands the plane atop the lorry's 40 ft container unit, which is travelling at a speed of 55 mph.

Lavatory – World Speed Record

In 1983, whilst waiting for another attempt at the world land speed record, Richard Noble and his team-sought diversionary amusement and set up the record for the world's fastest moving lavatory.

Towed behind a pick-up truck, this normally private piece of plumbing achieved a speed of 70 mph with an un-named team member squatted aboard.

Magic Square

A magic square is an arrangement of numbers in the shape of a square. Starting with the number one, a progression is made without omitting consecutive numbers. The numbers are arranged so that the sum of each horizontal row, each vertical column and each diagonal row are equal. The largest magic square ever was completed in 1975 by thirteen year old American Wayne Tulip. Each row added up to an amazing 578,865.

Alternative Fact

The first flush toilet on record is one discovered during excavations in Crete in 1899. Excavation leader Doctor Thomas Dunn dated the find, using similar artefacts discovered at Knossos, as over 4,000 years old.

Bigamy

On 31st December 1981, Florida police issued a statement to the effect that Giovanni Vigliotto, fifty-two, had admitted to no less than 82 bigamous marriages. Two of the marriages were made whilst cruising the Caribbean with a friend. He married two passengers in the space of three weeks. His eighty-third wife had no comment to make.

Orange – Oldest

Mrs Olive Wood of Derby claims the record for possessing the world's oldest orange. Now wizened and black, it was thrown off the *Lusitania* on her maiden voyage in 1912.

Musical Chairs

The world's largest ever game of musical chairs, involving 4,514 players, was won by Scott Ritter, aged eighteen, of Ohio State University on 25th April, 1982.

Paper Chain

By using 125,000 staples, children at Thorpe-le-Soken, Essex, made the world's longest ever paper chain of 8 miles 897 yards on 24th to 25th May, 1975 over a period of 24 hours.

ALTERNATIVE FACT

The honeymoon was originally a period of time when a groom had to hide his bride until her family grew tired of searching for her.

Pancake Tossing

On 26th February, 1974, Shrove Tuesday, Mrs Sally Cutter of Limasol, Cyprus achieved 5,010 tosses in 65 minutes, an average of one toss every 0.78 seconds.

Mary Kennedy, twenty-two, of Aylesbury, Bucks, managed 80 tosses in one minute on Shrove Tuesday, 1976, an average of one toss every 0.75 seconds.

Pancake Throwing

By using a secret thickening ingredient David Walsh is able to produce flexible (yet edible) pancakes $\frac{1}{4}$ inch thick. David then projects them like frisbees. His best throw achieved a distance of 58 ft 4 ins on 29th February, 1980.

Mouse Trap

The fastest-acting mouse trap ever made is the 'little nipper' manufactured by Messrs Proctor Bros of Bedwas, Gwent.

From the time the hungry mouse alights on the trap to the time the break-back arm snaps onto its unsuspecting victim is 10.38 milliseconds (a fraction more than one hundredth of a second).

Alternative Fact

People are still searching for a better mouse-trap. Up to 1st January, 1984 the Patents Office has listed no fewer than 294 different types and improvements of mouse-traps.

Oldest and Longest Serving Choirboy

On 26th June, 1983, Herbert Day of Colin St Dennis, Gloucester, celebrated two anniversaries.

On his 90th birthday, Herbert became the oldest serving choirboy in the world. And it marked his 85th continuous year as a chorister.

Nose Poking

As a protest against not having a clean handkerchief to go to school with, Paul Clarkson, fourteen, sat with the little finger of his right hand pushed up his left nostril for a period of 12 hours at his home in Solihull, Birmingham on 16th February, 1972.

Kissing – Duration

On Brighton pier, on 17th August, 1976, James Patterson and his girlfriend Toni Smith exchanged kisses at an average rate of one every 0.35 of a second. They continued embracing each other for a period of two hours to set a new world record of 20,010 kisses in this period.

ALTERNATIVE FACT

Contrary to rumour, Eskimos actually do kiss. The rubbing of noses is a sig of greeting and respect but Eskimo lovers kiss in exactly the same way as everyone else.

Motorcar – Long Distance

The longest non-stop distance ever covered by a motor-car is the 7,500 mile journey from Alaska to Mexico achieved by the Cadillac owned by American, Louis Mattar.

Specially adapted for long distance, non-stop travel the car features a bed, fridge, freezer, barbeque, washing machine, ironing board, bar, TV, telephone, toilet, shower and drinking fountain.

Retractable bogie wheels enable the car's road wheels and tyres to be changed on the move.

Up to March 1983 the car had covered a total of 460,000 miles on the same engine. The average fuel consumption is a mere 10 mpg.

Mouse Catching

The world-record-holding moggy for the most kills is Towser the twenty-year-old tortoiseshell cat from the Glen Turret Distillery, Crieff, Scotland.

To 30th June, 1983, Towser had amassed a total of 22,126 kills. These have been religiously recorded over the years by Peter Fairlie, the company's Sales Manager.

Towser keeps in trim with a daily dram of fifteen-year-old malt whisky.

Pea Pushing

A Derbyshire woman, Helen McDonald, set two world records for pea pushing on 14th February, 1970.

Using only her nose, she covered 100 yards in 4 minutes 30 seconds. Helen went on to complete 1 mile in 6 hours 40 minutes.

Oldest Man Alive

Apart from biblical characters, several legendary figures are claimed to have lived lengthy lives.

Islamic holy man, Sayed Abdul Mabood, has certified evidence (his passport) that he is over 160 years old. His date of birth is recorded as 13th December, 1823 and, according to officials it is no mistake!

Mr Mabood is a well-respected holy-man in his local community in Pakistan and has friends in government and religious circles. His eldest son is aged 100 and he is grandfather to more than 200 children.

Murderess – World's Most Determined

In January 1978 it was reported that an un-named thirty-six-year-old American woman was to be tried for the murder of her husband. Before finally succeeding, by dropping tranquilizers into his beer and smashing his skull with a steel weight, she first tried: Putting a large dose of LSD in his toast. Serving him with blackberry pie containing the venom sack of a tarantula spider. Placing bullets in the carburettor of his lorry. Tossing a live electric wire into his shower. Injecting air into his veins with a hypodermic needle to induce a heart attack.

Puzzle Ring

The fastest recorded time for reassembling an eight-stranded puzzle ring is 56 seconds, by Billy Wood of Baildon, West Yorkshire on 4th December, 1982 at the Queens Head public house, Burley in Wharfedale, Yorkshire.

Shaving

On 28th April, 1983 at Gillingham, Kent, Jerry Harley shaved 987 volunteers in 60 minutes using a well sharpened cut-throat razor.

Jerry uses the special 'three slash' technique taking a little over three seconds to complete each shave.

Alternative Fact

During the eighteenth century barbers used to perform minor operations as well as carry out their tonsorial duties.

The most comon of these operations was "blood-letting" whereby the patient was "bled" whilst holding on to a large pole standing in the shop. When not in use the pole was left standing by the shop door, draped in bandages as an advertisement of the barber's skills.

Barber's Pole

The world's tallest barber's pole, built in 1973 outside a shop in Alexander, New York, USA, stands 50 ft 3 ins high.

Trolly Pushing

On 18th July, 1977, Dave Patterson and Dave Brown alternately pushed a 'borrowed' supermarket trolly between Barnstaple, Devon and Taunton, Somerset, a distance of 53 miles. The journey took exactly 24 hours to complete and whilst one was pushing, the other sat in the trolly.

Trolly Standing

The greatest number of people to stand upright and unsupported in a "Hillards" supermarket trolly, for a period of not less than 30 seconds, is five, by a group of party-goers at Burley-in-Wharfedale, Yorkshire on 1st January, 1982.

Record Recognition

The only person to demonstrate his ability to correctly identify the name of a classical hi-fi record by merely looking at the groove pattern is Doctor Arthur Lindstrom of Philadelphia, USA. On some of the more popular records, Arthur can even name the orchestra, the conductor and at which studio it was made!

Train Travel

Senior citizen, Horace Pallen, sixty-six, of Shavington, Crewe, claims the record for the most use of a British Rail Awayday ticket. On 22nd November, 1982, Horace covered 1,328 miles.

Tiddlywink - High Jump

The greatest height to which a standard match-play tiddlywink has been flicked (over a bar to a measured height) is 54 ins by Robert Baistow and David Tomlinon in January 1983. The English Tiddlywink Association condemned the record as 'bringing the game into disrepute'.

Tiddlywink - Long Jump

The longest distance to which a standard match play tiddlywink is claimed to have been flicked is 3 metres 85 cm by Marie Junot of Abbe-ville, France on 22nd September, 1980. The distance was measured from the point of the flick to the nearest impression made in a garden sandpit.

Sheep to Suit

The shortest recorded time taken to transform the fleeces of three sheep into a suit of clothes has been achieved by a team from the Melbourne College of Textiles, Australia in 1 hour 34 minutes.

Sheep to Blanket

Ninety members of staff at Charles Early and Marriot Ltd., of Whitney, Oxfordshire produced fifty full sized blankets from fleece to finished dyed article in 14 hours 4 minutes. It took just 8 hours 11 minutes to complete the first blanket.

Spoon Hanging

Keeping her head at an angle of 90 degrees to her body and using a standard teaspoon, Ami Barwell aged five, of Hedon, Hull, Humberside, 'spoon-hung' for 2 hours 10 minutes continuously.

Space Hoppers – Highest

The greatest height ever cleared on a space-hopper is one of 30 ins by Janina Pulaski on BBC TV on 26th May, 1975.

Space Hopper - Fastest

The fastest recorded time taken to cover a measured 100 yards on a space hopper is 46.4 seconds by twelve year-old Daniel Evans of Southend, Essex on 19th September, 1975.

Sausage

The world's largest and heaviest sausage was made in Birmingham by Rex's Sausage Co. Ltd., between 19th and 21st June, 1983. Weighing in at 2.89 tonnes the $5\frac{1}{2}$ mile long sausage took ten hours to complete, spread over the three days.

The 160 lbs of seasoning needed was provided by the Hull firm of Spice Blenders Ltd.

Potatoes in a Bucket

At Perth, Western Australia on 6th May, 1968 Ivan Veriman (thrower) and Alexandra Crosby (catcher) successfully propelled ten full size potatoes a minimum distance of 100 ft into a 2½ gallon plastic bucket. The time taken was 2 minutes 33 seconds.

Tree Frog

The largest and heaviest arboreal amphibian (tree frog) ever known to exist is the Australian 'Hulk'.

Hulk lives with his owner, Steve Crabtree, thirty-seven, at Southsea, Hampshire.

In June 1983 'Hulk' measured 4½ inches long, 4½ inches across and weighed 7½ ounces.

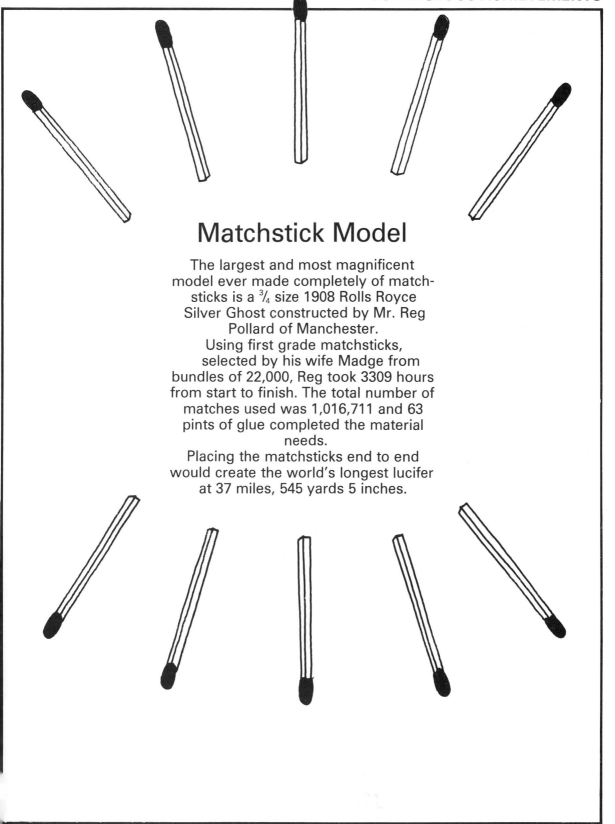

Matchstick Model

The largest and most magnificent model ever made completely of matchsticks is a ¾ size 1908 Rolls Royce Silver Ghost constructed by Mr. Reg Pollard of Manchester.

Using first grade matchsticks, selected by his wife Madge from bundles of 22,000, Reg took 3309 hours from start to finish. The total number of matches used was 1,016,711 and 63 pints of glue completed the material needs.

Placing the matchsticks end to end would create the world's longest lucifer at 37 miles, 545 yards 5 inches.

Truck Jumping

On 12th June, 1983, John 'Golly' Goddard, twenty-four, soared to a new world record on his 500 cc Kawasaki motor bike by successfully leaping over 15 trucks.

Golly's leap covered 162 ft and was performed in front of a crowd of 10,000 at Trentham Gardens near Stoke, Staffordshire.

Two-Wheel Drive

Driving an IVECO 190 Tractor unit (normally used for towing 40 ft 38 tonne trailers) French stunt driver Gilbert Bataille performed a record breaking 32-second run on only two wheels.

Surfing Rabbit

The world's first and only surfing rabbit is Hazel from Florida, USA who regularly hops aboard her own special miniature surfboard to frolic in the Atlantic Ocean.

Snake Sacking

In Bolivar, Pennsylvania, USA they practise the way-out sport of snake sacking.

Five rattlesnakes are tipped from a sack at the feet of the participant who then, with ungloved hands, has to grab the snakes and stuff them, head first, back into the sack which is held open by a colleague. The holder of the world record speed Snake Sacking record is Steve Ekenroad with a time of 5.5 seconds. Being bitten means disqualification.

Table – Most People On

A team of gymnasts from Arizona State University, headed by coach Don Robinson, succeeded in cramming 25 people on top of a table measuring 5 ft by 3ft. Just for fun, each gymnast had to mount the table by doing a forward somersault.

Table Lifting

Using only a firm grip on one of the four supporting legs, Alan Pickering of Darlington, Cleveland, claims he can lift a 2 ft diameter bar table weighing 28 lbs to the vertical 20 times in one minute.

Chair Lifting

Alan Pickering also claims he can lift a bar chair weighing $18\frac{1}{2}$ lbs to the vertical 25 times in one minute. Another of Alan's records is 200 lifts in 30 minutes and 310 in one hour.

Truck Pulling

Olympic shot-putter and The world's strongest man, Geoff Capes, holds the world record for truck pulling. Geoff pulled a $12\frac{1}{2}$ tonne juggernaut a distance of 25 metres in 54.3 seconds at the National Sports Centre, Crystal Palace, London.

Sausage Making

Dave Kersey of Grimsby, South Humberside, has laid claim to the title of World Champion Sausage Maker. From July 1975 to July 1983 Dave has regularly turned out 30,000 sausages every week, weighing more than 1½ tonnes. The composite total to 20th July, 1983 is 12,500,000.

Tea Making

On 28th September, 1983, eight-year-old Cub Scout, Tony Murray, of Barrow in Furness, Cumbria completed a 14-day tea making marathon.
Tony made a record of 2713 cups of tea in his allotted time.

Sahara Trek

With daytime temperatures reaching 120 degrees Farenheit, Ted Edwards, aged forty-four, of Eccles, Greater Manchester, became the first man to walk the 350 miles across the Sahara Desert's 'Empty Quarter'. Ted's epic journey took him 19 days to complete, starting from Mali and finishing in Mauretania.

Weight Gain

Between January 1982 and Christmas of the same year Sid Barrett of Plymouth increased his weight from 14 stone to 30 stone to win a £3,000 bet. This record is for information purposes only and is definitely not one to attempt to beat.

The heaviest human in medical history was John Minnoch of Washington, USA whose weight in March 1978 was stated by doctors at the University Hospital Seattle, USA to be in excess of 100 stone. It was reported in October 1981 that after coming off a strict diet he gained 14 stone in 7 days.

107

Weather Balloon – Inflating

The shortest time taken to inflate an 8 ft diameter weather balloon to its fullest extremity, using lung power, is 2 hours 56 minutes recorded by Mel Robson of Newcastle, Tyne and Wear, on 7th February, 1982.

Weddings

The record for the most weddings in a lifetime is held by King Mogut of Siam (of *The King And I* fame) who during his reign had no less than 9,000. This also meant that he had 9,000 wives!

Water Baling

This record is for the quickest time taken to bale a 'pond-sized' amount of water out of a single receptacle.

The gallonage is now set at 170 Imperial Gallons and the baling record, using a No 1 size thimble is held by 12 children of the Chesterfield Young Oxfam Group, who on 15th March, 1975, completed their task in twelve hours exactly.

Whip Cracking

In order to crack a whip, the tip must be made to travel faster than the speed of sound (1,000 ft per second).

The only man to ever crack a whip over 100 ft long is Australian Noel Harris. His record breaking whip measured 105 ft 4 ins and took the hides of three cows to make.

Whistling

The loudest recorded level at which a human being has whistled is 117 decibels, by Australian Steven West on 26th June, 1982.

Escapology

World famous escapologist Harry Houdini (born 1874 as Ehrich Weiss) performed a unique escape. He was sealed in a metal coffin which was then submerged under water. One hour and 42 seconds later he escaped and surfaced. Experts afterwards stated that they thought him dead, as the volume of air contained in the sealed coffin was only sufficient to sustain life for approximately 15 minutes.

Raffle Prize

The most valuable prize ever offered for a raffle is the 380-acre estate at Mullingar, Eire worth £1,500,000.

Raffle organiser and estate owner, Barney Curley, forty-four, sold 9,000 tickets at £175 each. The owner of the winning ticket was Mr Tony Ray of Tewkesbury, Gloucester who shared his prize with five friends when the draw took place on 9th February, 1984.

Wicker Basket

The world's largest wicker basket stands 18 ft high and 14 ft across. Made in Germany as a receptacle and display piece for cushions, it took eleven miles of wicker and osier to complete.

Worm Stuffing

The world record for Worm Stuffing (putting five innocent little earthworms into a sack held by a colleague) is 10.34 seconds by Barry Sheene (sack held by Jan Ravens) on Yorkshire Television's *Just Amazing* programme.

Tortoise – Multiple Birth

Mrs Chris Hall of Minster, Isle of Sheppey lays claim to a world record on behalf of her pet tortoises Kizzy and Hercules. Over a four week period ending on 6th February, 1984 Kizzy successfully hatched out 15 babies, including one set of twins.

Oldest Boss

The world's oldest company boss is Mary Moody, born on 7th April, 1881 who has been chairman of the Stourbridge printers, Mark and Moody, since 1926.

Marriage – Largest Age Difference

The greatest difference in age between marrying adults is 88 years in the case of Ali Azam, 104, and his bride, sixteen-year-old Maruim Begum.

Ali, as his title of Imam suggests, is a priest. They were married on 22nd April, 1983 in the village of Fateabad, Chittagong, Bangladesh.

Unfortunately the local villagers disapproved of the marriage because it was Ali's fifth, and under Islamic law he's only allowed a maximum of four. Ali explained that he had to marry the girl to save her from starving to death.

'Y' Front Leaping

The most number of times a pair of 'Y' front underpants have been donned and removed in one minute is 21 times. This was achieved by Frenchman Didier Le Camp on BBC Television's *Late, Late Breakfast Show* on 10th December, 1983.

Fastest Teddy Bear

Mr Whoppit, a teddy bear owned by the late Sir Donald Campbell, holds the world speed records for land and water. Whilst breaking and creating new land and water speed records, Sir Donald would always be accompanied by Mr Whoppit tucked safely under the seat.

On that fatal day of 14th January, 1967, Sir Donald's turbo jet-engined Bluebird K7 achieved a speed of 328 mph just prior to crashing.

Very little wreckage was ever recovered and the body of Sir Donald Campbell was never found. But floating and bobbing at the scene of the crash on Coniston Water, Cumbria was Mr Whoppit.

Cabbage – Tallest in World

The tallest cabbage ever grown was the 'Jersey' variety, reared by Mr John Black of Lancaster. On 15th April, 1983 the monster had reached 13 ft 1 ins in height.

General Election – Biggest Bet

On 18th May, 1983, an anonymous punter from the Cotswolds staked £90,000 on the Conservatives to win the election. The bet was placed at Corals in Fleet Street, London, at odds of 2 – 9. Directly after taking the bet, Corals dropped the odds to 1 – 6.

Worst Opening Sentence For A Novel

Launched in California, USA in February 1983, the well publicised competition for the world's worst opening sentence for a novel attracted over 10,000 entries from 50 countries.

Organised by Dr Scott Rice, professor of English at San Jose State University, the competition was named after Edward Bulwer Lytton, the Victorian author who began one of his 28 novels with the phrase: 'It was a dark and stormy night' and continued for a further 53 words with four commas, a dash and one set of brackets.

The competition was won by American Gail Scott. Miss Scott's winning entry was: 'The camel died suddenly on the second day and Selena fretted sulkily and buffing her already impeccable nails – not for the first time since the journey began – pondered snidely if this would dissolve into a vignette of minor inconveniences like all the other holidays spent with Basil'.

Wheelchair Marathon

The longest recorded distance ever travelled non stop by wheelchair was 100 miles. The record breakers were Andy Stoner, aged twenty-one, of Perranporth and Allan Wyle, aged nineteen, of Exeter who reached St Austell, Cornwall on 17th April, 1983. Both men are physically disabled and raised a commendable £2,500 for charity.

High Diving Priest

On 4th July, 1983 as part of a sponsored money-raising spectacle, seventy-year-old Abe Robert Simon, curate of Saone for 20 years, dived 55 ft from a cliff into a river. Abe Simon raised over £3,000 for charity.

Slate Smashing

Policeman Ian Womersley, aged twenty-four, of Hemsworth, Yorkshire set a new world record on 26th September, 1983 by consecutively smashing 403 slates with his feet.

Telephone Directory Tearing

The fastest recorded time measured to tear in half a telephone directory, minimum thickness 2 cm is 2.25 seconds by Alex Appleton of Tonbridge, Kent, on 18th June, 1974. Alex went on to set another world record by tearing in half 15 similar sized phone books in one minute.

Parsnip

The longest parsnip ever grown is one measuring 35 inches long from tip to head, by Andrew Skippines, of Ipswich, Suffolk. This was reported on 28th January, 1983.

Queueing

Philip Illsley, aged twenty-one, from Windsor holds the world record for queueing. From 13th to 28th December, 1983 (15 days) Philip queued outside the London store of Selfridges. During his lone vigil he was robbed, jeered and blown out of his sleeping bag by an IRA bomb. Philip's prize: a black and silver ballpoint pen reduced from £2.25 to £1.50.

Latrine Pit Digging

The fastest recorded time for digging a 2 metre deep, 5 metre long latrine pit is 72 hours by Mr July Nkomo of Mudiwie, Zimbabwe between 20th and 22nd April, 1982.

Sunflower – Most Blooms

The greatest number of flower heads to bloom simultaneously on a sunflower is 60, produced by a 9 ft 6 ins specimen grown by Mrs Lilly Chinery of Elveden, Lancashire during the summer of 1983.

Motorbike – Land's End to John O'Groats

On 2nd October, 1983, Tony Goulding, aged thirty-five, of Retford, Notts, claims to have set a new record by riding the 930 miles from Land's End to John O'Groats in 11 hours 58 minutes.

Piano Throwing (Male)

On 10th March, 1983, a team of 6 from Newcastle University set a world record for piano throwing of 11 ft 6$\frac{1}{2}$ ins during their Community Action Week of fundraising events.

Piano Throwing (Female)

Taking part in the same contest were six women, also from Newcastle University. Intent on setting a ladies' record, they unfortunately dropped the piano on the backswing thus setting a record of minus 1 ft 6 ins.

Piano Smashing

The record for smashing an upright piano into pieces small enough to be passed through a hoop 9 ins in diameter is 1 minute 37 seconds achieved by six members of the Tinwald Rugby Club, Ashbourne, New Zealand on 6th Novenber, 1977.

Rarest Toad

Now residing at the Natural History department of Rotherham Museum is Tommy, the rarest toad in the world.

Tommy is unique, for he is the only known albino toad ever to have existed. The museum curators are encouraging Tommy to mate and say that his pink eyes, cream coloured skin and deep pink warts should make him irresistible.

THE AMAZING PETER DOWDESWELL

Peter Dowdeswell is to eating and drinking as Torvill and Dean are to Ice Dancing; very rarely beaten. Peter lives with his wife Connie and three children in the town of Earls Barton, Northamptonshire. Also resident at the Dowdeswell household are two Dobermann Pinscher dogs, an Alsatian bitch, a very expensive Persian cat, a parrot, four ducks and a hare.

Not only does Peter feature as world champion 'trencherman' but the bug has bitten other members of the family,

namely wife Connie, son Tony and son-in-law Shaun Barry. Their feats are recorded in chapter 7.

In 1974, Peter Dowdeswell began his phenomenal record breaking career by downing a three pint yard of ale in an incredible 5.4 seconds. Since then Peter has travelled the world, breaking one record after another and raising thousands of pounds for charity. Up to 9th February, 1984, Peter's total sponsored earnings for charity amounted to almost £70,000. Many's the time this

six foot one, 16½ stone quietly spoken cockney has answered the challenge of would-be pretenders to his crown. All have been beaten into obscurity but all will remember Peter Dowdeswell.

Of the 196 world records Peter claims to hold, a selection are listed below.

Drinking

1 pint of beer in 0.45 seconds.
1 pint of beer upsidedown in 2.58 seconds.
1 litre of beer in 1.30 seconds.
1 litre of beer upsidedown in 6.0 seconds.
2 pints of beer in 2.30 seconds.
2 pints of beer upsidedown in 6.4 seconds.
2½ pint 'yard of ale' in 5.05 seconds.
3 pint 'yard of ale' in 5.40 seconds.
3 pints of beer in 4.2 seconds.
3½ pint 'yard of ale' in 8.20 seconds.
4 pints of beer upsidedown in 22.1 seconds.
2 litres of beer in 6.0 seconds.
2 litres of beer upsidedown in 15.2 seconds.
4 pint 'yard of ale' in 8.90 seconds.
5 pint 'yard of ale' in 10.00 seconds.
5 pints of beer upsidedown in 29 seconds.
7½ pint 'yard of ale' in 14 seconds.
One gallon of beer upsidedown in 8 minutes 35 seconds.
12 pints of beer whilst Big Ben is striking twelve. (Big Ben had only got to 9 before Peter had finished!!)
1 pint of champagne upsidedown in 3.3 seconds.
3½ pint 'yard of champagne' in 14.2 seconds.

2 pints of milk in 3.2 seconds.
34 pints of beer in 1 hour.
90 pints of beer in 3 hours.

In October, 1979, Peter was subjected to rigorous and exacting tests by the medical profession in order that they might discover why he never showed any signs of drunkeness after consuming so much alcohol during his world record breaking feats for charity.

Doctors hoped that by using Peter as 'guinea pig' they might find a cure for alcoholism.

Peter drank four pints of beer during an hour and was given a breathalyser test. The meter reading (50) indicated that his blood/alcohol level equated to the same as if he had consumed only one and a half pints of beer. During the next four hours Peter was asked to consume a further 21 pints of beer, which he obligingly did. This brought the total consumed to 25 pints in five hours. After every five pints Peter was given a breathalyser test and blood test. The meter reading of 50 never varied and the blood analysis confirmed that according to science he had only consumed the equivalent alcohol contained in one and a half pints of beer.

Undeterred, the scientists decided to try again to get Peter drunk and later during that same month of October, 1979 he was subjected to what must surely be the ultimate in medical research in alcohol consumption. Using the same methods as before and treble-checking all the equipment and findings, Peter consumed 76 pints of beer inside 16 hours of testing. On each and every occasion the result was the same.The instruments and blood

analysis showed a blood/alcohol level equivalent to Peter only having consumed one and a half pints of beer.

It is not known exactly how far the team of scientists have progressed since their findings were made public but it's a fair bet they are still as baffled as ever.

Eating

Doughnuts 113 single hole in 8 minutes 45 seconds.
Jelly 18 fluid oz in solidified form with a spoon in 22.34 seconds.
Meat Pies 22 5½ oz meat pies in 18 minutes 13.3 seconds.
Cheese 1 lb of cheddar in 1 minute 13 seconds.
Pancakes 62 6 inch diameter, buttered and with syrup, in 6 minutes 58.5 seconds.
Grapes 3 lb bunch (still attached to stalks) in 31.1 seconds.
Gherkins 1 lb in 27.2 seconds.
Strawberries 2 lb 8 oz in 27.19 seconds.
Shrimps 3 lb in 4 minutes 8 seconds.
Mashed Potato 3 lb in 1 minute 22 seconds.
Doughnuts 45 two-hole doughnuts in 17 minutes 32 seconds.
Eels 1 lb (elvers) in 13.7 seconds.
Eggs, raw 13 in 1.4 seconds.
Eggs, soft boiled 32 in 1 minute 18 seconds.
Eggs, hard boiled 14 in 58 seconds.
Prunes 144 in 53.5 seconds.
Haggis 1 lb 10 oz in 49 seconds.
Jam Sandwiches 40 6 ins x 3¾ ins x ½ ins in 17 minutes 53 seconds.
Porridge 6 lb in 2 minutes 34 seconds
Fish and Chips 4 lb fish plus 4 lb chips in 5 minutes 15 seconds.
Ice Cream (partly thawed) 12 lb in 45.5 seconds.
Spaghetti 100 yards in 21.7 seconds.

Peter reckons that his only key to success is by hard work and constant practice. 'The reason I drink beer so quickly is that I can't stand the taste,' he quips. Odd as that might sound, it's perfectly true, Peter is a tee-totaller and drinks only soft drinks when he's down at his local pub in Earls Barton, The Boat, unless he's breaking records.

The Landlord of The Boat doesn't mind that a bit, though, and lets Peter practice his drinking exercises in one of the back rooms, whenever there's a charity display coming up.

The following few records are also held by Peter Dowdeswell, but are for information purposes only and definitely not recommended to be attempted:

Eating 12 champagne glasses in 5 minutes.
Eating 4 packets of razor blades in 2 minutes 35 seconds.
Eating a 1 pint dimple beer mug in 3 minutes 45 seconds.

Peter described his most dangerous 'cabaret act' as 'strangulation'. A 20 ft piece of 1½ inch diameter rope is looped around his neck and tied in an overhand knot. Ten men, five at each side, then pull on both of the loose ends. Peter has been able to sustain breathing, by using only the strength of his throat and neck muscles, for a period of 15 minutes. Definitely not one for anybody to attempt.

GASTRONOMIC RECORDS

Compared to the titanic gastronomic achievements of Peter Dowdeswell the following list of eating and drinking records don't bear comparison. However, notoriety for all record-breakers is the theme of this book, so here goes:

Barrel of Beer

The shortest recorded time in which a 9-gallon barrel of hand-drawn ale has been consumed is 2 hours 52 minutes, by a team of six at the Queen's Head, Burley in Wharfedale, Yorkshire on 6th May, 1968.

Blood Alcohol Level

In December 1982, a twenty-four year-old Los Angeles woman was found to have 1,510 milligrams of alcohol per 100 millilitres of blood in her body.

She is still alive and none the worse for wear but doctors state that the 'death level' is usually around 400 milligrams.

This record is for information only and should definitely not be attempted.

ALTERNATIVE FACT

If all the blood vessels in an adult human being were straightened out and placed end to end, they would be 100,000 miles long; long enough to go round the Earth four times.

Beer Through a Straw

The fastest recorded time that a pint of beer has been drunk through a straw (no more than 3 mm in diameter) is 25.07 seconds by Patrick Tyler, aged thirty-two, at the Ponsmere Hotel, Perranporth, Cornwall on 14th July, 1983.

Beer with a Teaspoon

Geoff Harding, aged nineteen, claims to have drunk a pint of beer using only a teaspoon in 2 minutes 54 seconds at the Red Lion, Manchester on 1st April, 1982.

ALTERNATIVE FACTS

In Sweden, being caught driving whilst under the influence of drink or drugs, brings a penalty of PERMANENT loss of licence.

In El Salvador the deterent is even greater. You could receive the DEATH PENALTY!

Foxy Boozer

A young fox cub kept by Ralph Barnett of Little Downham, Cambridgeshire, holds the foxy boozer record for drinking half a pint of beer, from a bowl, in 43 seconds.

Grass Eating

After losing a bet to a fellow young farmer, Paul Shaw of Swindon, Wiltshire was forced to pay the penalty. He ate 16 ounces of fresh grass-mowings, using only a knife and fork, in exactly 15 minutes on 22nd May, 1968.

Hamburgers

The world record for eating 4 oz hamburgers stands at 25 in 30 minutes achieved by Stuart Haig of Sheffield, Yorkshire in July, 1983.

Lager Through a Straw

The fastest recorded time that a pint of lager has been drunk through a straw (no more than 3 mm in diameter) is 32.9 seconds by Paul Cairns, aged eighteen, at the Ponsmere Hotel, Perranporth, Cornwall on 13th July, 1983.

Peas – Tinnned

Alan Evans of Hull, East Yorkshire has laid claim to this record by eating almost three medium sized tins of gardens peas individually with a cocktail stick in 1 hour on 15th August, 1973.

Future record attempts will be accepted for a maximum consumption in a 30 minute period or the shortest time taken to devour 500 peas.

Oysters

The most prodigious feat of consuming shelled oysters was achieved by Australian Ron Hansen on 30th June, 1982. At the Packers Arms Queenstown, New Zealand, he slurped 250 of them down his gullet in 2 minutes 52.3 seconds.

Pineapple

The fastest recorded time for devouring a 2 lb pineapple, skin and all (but not the green top), is 3 minutes 33.4 seconds by Dave Walton of Newcastle, Tyne and Wear, on 17th December, 1974.

Sultanas

The fastest recorded time that 100 sultanas have been devoured, singly, using only a cocktail stick, is 2 minutes 25.39 seconds by Luke Barwell, aged ten, of Hedon, Hull on 14th September, 1983.

Sausages

In January 1983, Joe Blackie of Edinburgh ate $122\frac{1}{2}$ average-size, cooked sausages in one hour at his local pub The Norhet.

Joe raised hundreds of pounds in sponsorship money for the local old folk to enjoy Burns' Night celebrations.

Cockles

2 pints in 2 minutes 00.4 seconds by Tony Dowdeswell, of Earls Barton, Northants, at the Corby Stardust Bingo Hall on 14th February, 1984.

Dog (Chow) Meat

At the Happy Valley Football Stadium, Hong Kong, on 19th September, 1980, Lim Ho Wong is reported to have consumed $3\frac{1}{2}$ lbs of cooked dog-meat in 18 minutes 10 seconds.

Earthworms

The greatest number of cooked worms (killed by chloroform and boiled for 15 minutes) to be eaten is 50 in 15 minutes by Darren Belcher, aged sixteen, of Cheltenham, Gloucester-shire, on 24th September, 1979.

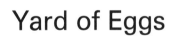

Yard of Eggs

In November 1982 on BBC Television, Geoff Derek of Sheffield drank 24 raw eggs from a yard of ale glass in 50 seconds.

Geoff would have done it much quicker, but at the time he was suffering from a bout of hiccoughs.

Port

Reports from various sources claim that at a charity banquet in London, Dr Samuel Johnson drank 36 glasses of port – without leaving the table once!

Snails

Frenchman Marc Quinquandon, aged twenty-seven, set a world record for eating snails on 25th November, 1979.

He consumed 72 in 3 minutes. Unfortunately some of them were toxic, which resulted in his collapse and death shortly thereafter.

Beer

The following records for consumption of beer by a woman are held by Mrs Connie Dowdeswell of Earls Barton, Northants:
1 pint of beer in 2.1 seconds.
1 pint of beer upsidedown in 5.2 seconds.
$3\frac{1}{2}$ pint 'yard of ale' in 12.00 seconds.

Chicken Eating

The fastest recorded time taken to consume 3 lb 12ozs of chicken meat (boneless) is 13 minutes 30 seconds, by Shaun Barry, aged twenty, of Earls Barton, Northants, at the Cardinal Wolsey Hotel, London, on 26th January, 1984.

Ice Cream Eating

The shortest time taken to eat 3lb 6 ozs of un-melted solid ice cream with a spoon is 50.3 seconds by Tony Dowdeswell, aged eighteen, at The Boat public house, Earls Barton, Northants.

Maggots

The fastest recorded time taken to eat 100 live maggots, individually without a drink (or being sick) is 6 minutes 15 seconds, by Arthur Morris, aged twenty-eight, of Greenock, Glasgow on 14th October, 1976.

Grass Eating (2)

According to information received from the *China Daily* on 26th January, 1983, farmworker Gong Qinqiao is addicted to grass.

He munches it every day at meal-times and gets a splitting headache when he stops.

Doctors report from his home in Eastern Sichuan that Gong is quite normal mentally but that his peculiar diet was gradually sapping his strength.

Monsieur Mangetout

Frenchman Michel Lotito uses the name 'Monsieur Mangetout' (Mr Eat-all) to describe quite aptly his feats of gastronomical omnivorousness.

Since he was sixteen, Michel has astounded friends and his doctors by eating:
7 bicycles
7 TV sets
80 ft. of steel chain
1 supermarket trolley in 4½ days
1 Cessna light aircraft in two years.
The metal was all ground into filings and the rubber and plastic chopped up and boiled before being swallowed. Another record that no one is recommended to challenge!

ALTERNATIVE FACTS

By the time most people are seventy they have chomped their way through a farmyard and a corner shop. According to the British Nutritional Foundation they will have eaten:
3 cows
17 pigs
420 chickens
4 miles of sausages
3,500 loaves of bread
4 tons of potatoes
2240 bags of crisps
2 tons of green vegetables.
To wash it all down they will have drunk:
93,000 cups of tea
910 gallons of beer.

THE DENBY DALE PIE

The largest pie ever made was produced in 1964 at the Yorkshire village of Denby Dale, to celebrate four royal births.

Here follows an account penned by the Committee Chairman, Mr John Hinchcliffe.

The first pie recorded in local history is that of 1788 which celebrated George III's recovery from illness. This recovery was, in fact, temporary, and he was troubled by mental affliction for the rest of his days.

However, many people believe that even before this date, pies were eaten in Denby Dale to celebrate great events, local or national. It is also said

that in those times great puddings were made, and that the local dignitaries ate the pie whilst the rest made do

with the more humble pudding. Certainly, puddings were eaten in surrounding villages on similar occasions, particularly at Clayton West, and local place names such as Pudding Mill reflect this.

Little is known of the 1788 pie other than that it was eaten in Cliffe Stile field on a hill on the outskirts of Denby Dale. By contrast a great deal is known about later pies. Victory Pie, celebrating the defeat of Napoleon by the Duke of Wellington at Waterloo in 1815, is the first for which a recipe survives. Positively lilliputian by later standards, it was baked in a kiln at the Corn Mill, Denby Dale, and contained half a peck of flour, two sheep and twenty fowls.

The third pie, and the only one to have a definite political association, celebrated the repeal of the Corn Laws.

This pie which, like the pies of 1887 and 1896, was baked in a circular dish, and contained:

5 sheep
1 calf
100 lbs of beef
7 hares
14 rabbits
2 brace of partridge
2 brace of pheasant
2 ducks
2 geese
2 turkeys
2 guinea fowls
4 hens
6 pigeons
63 small birds (their kind was unspecified)

The crust:
44¹/₂ stones of flour
9¹/₂ lbs lard
16 lbs butter.

Like its successor of 1887, the recipe seems to have been a matter not so much of planning, as of shooting everything in Denby Dale except people and horses.

Thirteen horses drew this giant pie around the village and we are told that three bands marched in the procession playing music. One can only hope that they either took turns to regain their wind or that, alternatively, they had practised together. Before the ceremony of the cutting of the pie could begin, the stand was pushed over by the disorderly crowd and the pie was tipped all over the field. Many people, however, are reported to have eaten pie from the ground where it fell.

In 1887 Queen Victoria was enjoying her Golden Jubilee and to mark this occasion Denby Dale baked another pie, a bigger and better one of course.

W. C. Holmes and Co., Gasometer makers of Huddersfield, made a round dish of riveted sheet steel weighing fifteen hundredweight. J. Drake and Sons of Halifax built an oven from 5,000 firebricks. Mr Joseph Barraclough made a boiler for the pre-cooking and F. Workman and Sons, who were employed to supervise the cooking, hired a London chef for the project. On the night before pie day this same chef caught a train back to the capital. This was perhaps not to be wondered at, for when the pie was opened it proved to be so bad that the 15,000 people who attended the ceremony rushed away from the terrible smell.

A little over a week later the women of Denby Dale made another pie. One must admire the extraordinary determination of these ladies who were rolling up their sleeves to make a 'resurrection pie' before their men-folk had completed the burial of its predecessor. This fifth pie set a precedent by eschewing all game, though it appears probable that the bad pie 'turned' as a result of allowing the meat to cool between the boiler and the dish. This 'resurrection pie' was eaten in Inkerman Hill, Denby Dale, on 3rd September, 1887, just across the road from Inkerman Park where all subsequent pies have been consumed.

It has been said with some justification that the sixth pie of 1896 had a somewhat weak 'raison d'etre'. Be that as it may, jubilees were rather in the fashion and the jubilee of the repeal of the Corn Laws did celebrate an event of national importance. The dish the pie was baked in on this occasion was the same one which had been used for two previous pies. In September 1940, during the scrap metal drive, the dish was auctioned and re-auctioned, then handed over for melting down for munitions.

The 1896 pie contained:
1,600 lbs of beef
270 lbs of veal
170 lbs of mutton and lamb
24 lbs of lard
24 lbs of butter
30 lbs of suet
20 stones of flour.

The seventh pie was baked on 4th August 1928, and little effort was made to tie this in with any great occasion, though some people maintain that its purpose was to celebrate the end of the First World War ten years earlier.

This may not be quite as far-fetched as it may sound – after all the conditions of austerity in 1953 stopped the projected baking of a pie to celebrate the Coronation of Queen Elizabeth II.

Whatever the 1928 pie was baked to celebrate, the purpose is well known: this was to raise £1,000 for the Huddersfield Royal Infirmary. In this endeavour the makers were wholly succesful, and in fact raised £1,062. 3s. 5d. for the Infirmary, and £85 for the local charities. Some £12 was raised by the player of a barrel organ, and almost £20 by the sale of poetry and songs of bygone pies, including some topical compositions lauding the 1928 venture.

The 1964 pie contained the following ingredients:

3 tons of prime English beef
$1\frac{1}{2}$ tons potatoes
$\frac{1}{2}$ ton of gravy and seasoning
$\frac{1}{2}$ ton of flour
$\frac{1}{4}$ ton of lard

The total volume for the pie was 162 cubic feet.

PUB GAMES & PASTIMES

Whilst traditional pub games and pastimes have been pushed into second place by the electronic machine, there are still a few eccentrics who carry on regardless. As well as the more recognised activities which take place in the hostelries of the world I have also included some of the more unusual.

Beer Mat Flipping

There have been many claims for records within this category, which now require standardization.

The beer mats must be square in shape, approximately 10 centimetres square.

The mats must only revolve half a turn after being flipped from the edge of a bar or table, before being caught in the same hand, with the fingers on top; thumb underneath in a pincer position.

Records based on the above rules are required for :
1) Right hand flipping
2) Left hand flipping
3) Simultaneous flipping with both hands.

Bottle Stretching

The largest distance ever stretched placing a half pint beer bottle to its furthest point is 8 ft 5½ ins by Ken Smith at the Jolly Pirate pub in Falmouth, Cornwall, on 20th August, 1978.

Darts High Score Marathon

The highest score ever attained in 24 hours non-stop play was 1,487,741 on a 'treble' board by a team of 12 from the Humber Bridge Hotel, Hessle, Hull, on 30th December, 1981. Each team member's average equated to 5165.78 per hour.

Darts – Best Average Over 24 Hours

Between 26th and 27th May, 1981, eight players from the Royal Hotel, Newsome, Huddersfield, scored a total 1,358,731 in 24 hours.

The average hourly score for each team member was 7076.72

Darts – Least Number to 1,000,000

The least number of darts taken to score one million is 39,566 by a team of eight players from The Sir John Barleycorn, Bitterne, Hampshire in a little over 36 hours between 4th and 6th April, 1980.

Potato Snooker

Using a harmless raw potato as the cue ball, Gary Milner and Stuart Allerston played one frame of snooker in 1 hour 13 minutes at the Birkholme Country Club, Hedon, Humberside on 4th February 1983.

Alternative Fact

The first ever match was developed by a group of French chemists in 1780. Unfortunately they forgot that one of the main ingredients comprising the head of the match was Phosphorous, a strong chemical poison, which resulted in two of the team dying from the inhalation of the toxic fumes.

The safety match was invented in 1827 by John Walker, an English pharmacist.

Match Flicking

The greatest horizontal distance that anyone has flicked a standard 'lucifer' is 27 ft 4 in by Mike Barwell at the British Legion Club, Hedon, Humberside on 24th December, 1981.

Match Striking

The contrived record for individually striking 48 standard matches is 52.2 seconds by Dennis Briggs at the British Legion Club, Hedon, Humberside on 24th December, 1981.

Public House – Longest Name

On Wednesday 29th June, 1983, in West Chelsea, London, a pub was opened called The Ferret and Firkin in the Balloon up the Creek. The name contains a total of 40 letters making it the longest pub name in the world.

The pub, owned by David Bruce, owes its name to a combination of events. Formerly called the Balloon Tavern, the locals hoped for a part of that name to be retained; The Ferret and Firkin was the name originally chosen by David Bruce, and the extra adjectives and adverbs were added as a description of the view from the pub which overlooks the upper reaches of Chelsea Creek.

Public Houses – Most Visits (ii)

Gastronome Jimmy Young G.M. B.E.M. claimed to have visited 23,338 different pubs up to 1st November, 1983.

Public Houses – Most Beers Sampled

In a career spanning 15 years George Morgan, aged thirty-five, from Luton, Bedfordshire claims to have visited 5,444 different pubs, sampling one pint of beer in each each. To 1st January, 1984, George had sampled 163 different types of draft beer and lager and 81 different types of bottled beers, lager and stout.

COLLECTING

The British are a nation of hoarders!

No, it wasn't Napoleon or Hitler who said that, it's just an opinion.

People everywhere collect things. From butterflies to badgers. From aardvarks to zips.

I want to hear about the things you collect, the zanier the better. Just for starters here are a few examples.

Tea Labels

In September 1964, Lyons launched a competition to promote sales of their Premium Tea.

In order to cover every permutation of the possible answers in the competition, the University of Sussex Union collected 1,440 Lyons Tea labels. On 5th October, 1964 their efforts were rewarded when they received first prize in the competition – a 1936 Vintage Fire Engine.

The Fire Engine was used for charitable purposes, giving outings to underpriviledged children and Old Age Pensioners.

Animals

The largest collection of 'wild' animals, numbering 5,100, are housed in the San Diego Zoo, California, USA.

Blowlamps

The largest known collection of blow-lamps is housed in the Garibaldi public house, Upper Bourne End, Buckinghamshire.

To 12th September, 1983, the total was 29, all different.

Marbles

Sam McCarthy of Southgate, Sussex has laid claim to the world's largest private collection of marbles.

To 19th September, 1983, Sam had amassed a varied assortment totalling 3,010. Doesn't seem many, does it? Can you beat it?

Packaging Collection

The largest assortment of collective packaging is one hoarded over the past 21 years by Londoner Robert Opie. Robert now never throws anything away for fear that a piece of important history will be lost forever.

To date Robert's collection comprises more than 250,000 items ranging from sweet wrappers through Cocoa tins and includes some 5,000 yoghurt pots.

Pigs

Mary Marsh of Edmondsham, Dorset, has the world's largest collection of piggy things.

To 19th October, 1983, her collection totalled 396, including such items as piggy banks, jugs, toys, biscuit barrels, soap dishes, and post cards.

ALTERNATIVE FACT

A person who collects piggy things is called a porcinologist.

Royal Memorabilia

The home of Mr and Mrs Hirst in Lancaster, Lancashire, houses the world's largest private collection of Royal memorabilia. Mrs Lesley Hirst started collecting after watching the Coronation on TV in 1953. To date her collection comprises 600 books, 230 pieces of chinaware, 500 postcards, 200 pitkins (small illustrated books) and numerous assorted coins, slides and magazines.

Beer Labels

The largest reported collection of all British Beer labels is one of 22,010 by Keith Osbourne of London.

Beer Can Tops

It has been reliably reported that the world's largest collection of beer can tops (ring pulls) is one amassed since 4th July, 1969 by the abstemious Arthur J. Jordan of Yorkstown, Virginia, USA. Arthur estimates the number conservatively at 710,500. Linked 'loop to curl' the tops stretched over $11\frac{1}{2}$ miles in length on 1st January, 1984.

Chimney Pots

The world's largest collection of assorted chimney pots is one numbering 50, gathered by Geoff Weaver of Nercwys, Mold. Geoff is currently building up a catalogue of his collection and would like to hear from other collectors world wide.

GCEs

Albert F. Prime collects GCEs like most people collect postage stamps. Albert, a prisoner at H.M. Open Prison, Sudbury, accumulated 34 'O' levels, 14 'A' levels and 1 'S' level (a total of 49) between 1968 and 1982.

Cactii

The world's largest collection of cacti, outside botanical gardens, is owned by Charles Abbott of Exeter, Devon. At 1st December, 1982, Charles' collection totalled 8,000. After a winter in the greenhouse, Charles takes his cacti off to his hairdressers for a shampoo and trim before showing them.

Key-Rings

The world's largest collection of key-rings is one gathered by Mr Tracey White of Daytona, Whittington, Salop, who to 26th August, 1983 had amassed 2,042, all different.

ALTERNATIVE FACT

The official name given to one who collects key-rings is a Copoclepholo-gist.

Dockland Treasures

The largest and most varied collection of bygone dockland equipment, outside a national museum, is housed at the barber's shop of Mr W. Oglesby of Hedon Road, Hull.

With the decline of the shipping trade to the port of Hull over the past few years, Mr Oglesby has amassed a vast collection of memorabilia and tools, etc., once used by the dockers and stevedores.

Apart from several hundred photographs, some dating back as far as 1880, Mr Oglesby's barber's shop is bedecked with 31 different types of bag hooks, 50 assorted hand hooks and a vast array of blocks, spades, shovels, sieves, satchels, tomahawks, ropeworkings and scoops.

Stamps

The greatest private stamp collection ever amassed was the one auctioned on 7th December, 1968 belonging to Josiah K. Lilley of Indianapolis, Indiana, USA. It has never been disclosed exactly how many individual stamps were included in the collection but the total money raised from the auction exceeded three million one hundred thousand dollars (approx. £1,310,000 at that date).

Autographs

The largest collection of autographed photographs signed by celebrities is one of 1,660 amassed by Peter Clark of London to 1st January, 1984.

Peter's collection contains several unique shots of man's first moon landing in 1969, all signed by the Apollo astronauts.

ACKNOWLEDGEMENTS

Mr Keith Harvey. A.R.S.H., R.P.

Mirror Group Newspapers.

The Daily Mail.

The Hull Daily Mail.

The University of Newcastle.

The University of Liverpool.

Nick Lord - Yorkshire Television.

Spice Blenders Limited.

Princess Royal Hospital, Hull.

Glen Turret Distillery.

The University of Sussex.

The British Nutrition Foundation.